PALESTINE-ISRAEL
One Democratic State?

A selection of statements and proposals made to the
United Nations in 1947
edited by Daniel Sochor, BA, JD

There is always hope when people are forced to listen to
both sides; it is when they attend only to one that errors
harden into prejudices.

John Stuart Mill, *On Liberty*

CONTENTS

I

Mr. EL-KHOURI [Representative of Syria to the United Nations]: ... I should like to explain to the General Assembly what the position of Syria is with respect to Palestine. I think most of you, if not all, know that Palestine used to be a Syrian province. Geographical, historical, racial and religious links exist there. There is no distinction whatever between the Palestinians and the Syrians and, had it not been for the Balfour Declaration and the terms of the mandate [*see* Appendix], Palestine would now be a Syrian province, as it used to be. Syria is intimately connected with Palestine, and is concerned with Palestinian questions more than any other State in the world. For this reason, you will excuse the Syrian delegation if, from time to time, it tries to explain its great concern and tells you of the danger facing Palestine and to what extent the Syrian delegation can resist that danger.

Had it not been for the Balfour Declaration and the insertion of that Declaration in the mandate, there would have been no problem of Palestine. The present problem is occupying and engaging the whole world. It is considered a complicated problem. Why? Let us find out who is responsible for creating this problem for the United Nations and for the whole world. I would appeal to your honesty and your loyalty. Are the Arabs responsible for that problem? Have they acted in any way or helped in any way to create such a problem? Certainly the answer to that question is no. The Arabs were living peacefully and quietly in their country and awaiting the result of the First World War in order to get their independence, according to the promises that had been made to them, just like any other nation of the world. What was intended was altogether different. A certain scheme, a certain conspiracy was hatched in

London or somewhere else. It was tried first in Berlin but it did not succeed there. Then new means were suggested in order to obtain the Balfour Declaration. The land and property of others was promised to a new foreign element who were to come to Palestine and establish themselves there and become a majority, dominating the country and removing the inhabitants from their homes.

We do not understand with what sort of mentality, with what logic, or what morals such a thing could be admitted or accepted by any civilized nation or any civilized person inspired by justice and reason.

Palestine is not an empty country; it is full. Let us see who the Palestinians are who are now called the Arabs of Palestine. It is a fact which some of you may or may not know.

The Palestinian Arabs are the descendants of the same inhabitants of that country of forty centuries ago who fought in the first campaign which the Jews waged against Palestine in the fifteenth century before Christ. In the Bible, they are called the Philistines. After about the thirteenth century, they adopted the Arabic language, which was later replaced by the Syrian language, a language closely related to the former. These people have not changed. They are the same people who were living there then. They have been there for forty centuries—since prehistoric times.

I have heard many references to the historical rights of the Jews in Palestine. I am sorry to say that I have heard them from persons who are well-learned and who know what is the truth. Those of you who have had a chance to read the Bible may find the history of the Jews in it. I do not need to give you a summary of the Bible but if you refer to it–those who believe in it and who have it–you will find the history of the Jews there. In the first place they came from Egypt on their return to Palestine. They came in spite of the Government of Egypt because they said they were enslaved there and they were molested by the Egyptian Government.

Well, if you read your Bible, you will find that the Pharaoh of Egypt said, in substance, to his ministers and to his people: "See, the children of Israel here are multiplying. There is a great fear that if war should come, they will join our enemy and fight against us. Let us manage it so that we can prevent any future difficulties with this people." It is in the Bible.

You will find that their persecution was not on any religious basis or because they had a faith. It was on a political basis and it is now the same thing. Then, under the guidance of Moses, and afterwards, under the guidance of Joshua and the other judges and kings, they started to invade Palestine and occupy certain portions of it with the policy of exterminating everybody there–men, women, children, old and young, even the animals–in order not to leave any trace of the living population of that country; and the places which they succeeded in conquering were so dealt with "to" utter destruction and extermination.

I do not tell you anything which is derived from any human historical source. It is all in the Bible. Before dealing with this problem, before thinking of the Jewish historical rights in Palestine, I invite you and request you to go and read your Bible. Everything there is clearly and definitely explained.

The Jews remained for a very short time in Palestine. They occupied the eastern portion of it. The western portion of Palestine–and the best part of it–was still occupied and held by the Philistines, the remote fathers of the present people of Palestine.

At last, the Jewish dynasty was abolished. It was done the first time by a Syrian emperor and the second time by Nebuchadnezzar, the Babylonian emperor, who deported the Jews to Persia and Mesopotamia where they remained for about seventy or eighty years.

There is one thing here which is very important. There are some religious people who refer to the prophecies in the Bible that the Jews will be restored to Palestine and to Jerusalem. Yes, it is true there are prophecies. But where are these prophecies? They occurred during the first captivity of the Jews when they were carried to Mesopotamia and the East. Then, the prophets appeared–Jeremiah, Ezekiel, Daniel, Isaiah–and said that God would have mercy on these people. He would have them returned to Jerusalem to build a world and build the Temple of God. The prophecies were made during that captivity. They were fulfilled. When Cyrus, the Persian emperor, took over the authority of Palestine from the Babylonians, according to the law of the Medes and the Persians which changeth not, according to the text of the Bible, he said that the Jews should be helped to return to Jerusalem and build the Temple of their God. That order was given to all his vassals and captains all over the East. Under the weapons and power of the great emperor of the East, they were allowed to come back.

At other times you will find it stated quite clearly in the Bible that the Arab prince Jasham resisted that order and he fought against it. But what could he do against the tremendous force of the Persian emperor at that time? The Jews succeeded in establishing themselves there under the authority of the Persians, and they continued as a Persian province until the invasion of the Macedonian emperor, Alexander the Great, in the fourth century B.C. They then became a Macedonian province, under the control of the Macedonians. They continued as such until the time of the Roman Empire, and then they remained among the Romans until the year 70 A.D. when Titus, the Roman, observing their disloyalty to the Roman Empire and the fact that they were so troublesome, decided to disperse them. He launched an invasion, destroyed their city and massacred them. Their remnants were dispersed all over the world. Most of them took refuge in Arabia, in the Hejaz and Yemen, and today there are remnants in Yemen and in the Arab territories.

Titus issued a decree to the effect that no Jew should enter Jerusalem. That decree continued in force during the Byzantine period, until the seventh century A.D., when the Arab, Omar Ibn Al-Khattab, came and invaded that country and wrested it from the Byzantine Empire–not from the Jews. Then the Christians of Jerusalem and their patriarch came to the caliph and said to him: "We have this decree from the Roman emperor that no Jew should be allowed to enter Jerusalem. We request that you respect that decree, and that it be kept in force." The caliph gave an order that it should continue in force, and it did so continue for a long period until the time of the Ottoman Empire when the Turkish rulers were paramount there. There was then a certain easy-going tolerance about the matter, and a few Jews did sneak in to Jerusalem from time to time.

This state of affairs continued for four centuries. The Jews had about 50,000 people in Palestine, and no more.

Now we come to the point at which Zionism was established at the end of the last century. The founder of Zionism was a certain Dr. Herzl. You know the Zionist programme is quite clear, and we are thankful to the representatives of the Jewish Agency for having come to the First Committee and having declared their case openly, frankly and boldly. They have said, "Our programme is this: we will have continuous, unlimited immigration into Palestine until we become a majority and dominate the country. We promise that the Arabs there will have fair play."

We thank them for that–that they will treat us fairly there–not only in Palestine, but in the neighbouring countries as well.

The first step that Dr. Herzl took was to go to Constantinople and to begin making arrangements with the Sultan of Turkey, Abdul Hamid. You have all heard of Abdul Hamid and know who he was. He was the absolute ruler of the huge Ottoman Empire, and he had full authority to do whatever he liked there. Dr. Herzl asked the Sultan, by promising him millions of pounds, to allow Jewish immigration into Palestine, in order to establish a Jewish national home there. The Sultan said to the people who approached him as intermediaries in this purpose, "Go and tell Dr. Herzl that I will not give one square foot of Palestine to the Jews. It is not my own property, but the property of my subjects who fertilized it with their blood. Let the Jews keep their millions for themselves." This was said by Abdul Hamid who was the absolute ruler of the country and who had authority for doing so. He could have done anything and invested it with legality.

How absurd it would be for an outsider who had

nothing to do with Palestine, who had neither subjects nor people there, to go and give definite promises to people all over the world that he would provide a national home for them in Palestine. Lord Balfour did it, I am sorry to say, and thereby he went beyond accepted limits.

I have talked about the Arabs of Palestine and of their descent. Now I want to know who are the Jews who want to establish a State for themselves in Palestine. Are they the Children of Israel as they claim? I say no. Very few of them are the Children of Israel. The Children of Israel are those Jews who are in the Arab world, in North Africa, in Syria, in Iraq, in Yemen and other places, and some of them in Western Europe and in America. They are also in Eastern Europe. Well, who are the Jews of Eastern Europe? I think you will have had a chance to know, and if you did not know it before, I refer you to the Jewish Encyclopaedia. You will find there the history of the Jews of Eastern Europe. They are Mongols who were near the Aral Sea, north of the Caspian Sea, and they had principalities there which were very strong in historical times. They established a dynasty which remained for a very long time. They were pagans at first but, in the seventh or eighth century after Christ, their prince said, "Paganism is useless. It is shameful for us, at this time, to be pagans. Let us adopt one of the heavenly religions, Christianity, Judaism or Islam."

He called three priests or bishops, one of each religion, and began to argue with them to find out about their religions in order to choose one of them. They argued between themselves before him. No one could convince the other or convince the prince that his religion was the better one. Then he decided to try another procedure. He was able at contriving procedures, and using them in his own interests.

He called each one of them alone. He called the Christian bishop and said to him, "If you were not a Christian, or if you were obliged to give up Christianity what religion would you be converted to, to Islamism or Judaism?" He thought a little and then said, "If I were to give up Christianity, I would become a Jew." He said he chose Judaism.

The prince called the follower of Islam and asked him the same question, and he also chose Judaism. He asked the Jew the same question. In reply, the Jew said, "I would kill myself and not adopt either of the other two religions."

He then found that there were three votes for Judaism and no votes for the other religions, so he declared Judaism to be the national religion and inculcated it in all his people. Judaism was established under the Khazar dynasty which lasted for several centuries in the southern part of Russia. When the Russian Empire came into being and could assume a position of power, it wanted to liquidate these principalities.

The Jewish dynasty was attacked and defeated, that is, those large groups of the Khazar people who were scattered in Russia, in Eastern Europe, throughout Poland, Romania and Odessa. That would explain why this group, this majority, would have been much greater numerically had it not been massacred from time to time and molested to such an extent that it could not multiply as it would have multiplied had it been treated differently in that country.

Now they want to have some place in the world where they can establish themselves as a State. Dr. Herzl had the happy idea of going back to Palestine to disturb that country which had been so calm, so tranquil, and so peaceful all the time, to stir up the area, and that state of affairs is continuing as you know. This is the situation as it now exists.

I shall turn now to the other point, namely, that Syria, as I said, is the motherland of Palestine. The Syrians believed that Palestine would be separated from Syria to form an independent State for the Palestinians themselves, not to be granted as a gift or as a present to a foreign people, in order that they should come to Palestine and dominate the people of that country and furthermore put pressure upon, endanger, and threaten the political, economic and social interests of the neighbouring countries, with Syria becoming the first sufferer in that respect.

We cannot admit that Palestine should not be granted its independence. We have voted against the terms of reference of the special committee because no mention was made in the terms of reference to the word "independence". I am sorry some of the speakers in the Committee avoided the word "independence" as if it were something injurious or as if it were out of order, claiming that it would prejudge the action of the special committee. We said that it would not prejudge action. This is the essential and the sole object of the mandate, that it be ended by independence, and by the termination of an unworkable mandate. It is the general principle of all mandates and trusteeships, that the end in view be independence. It is in the Charter and the Covenant of the League of Nations [*see* Appendix].

Should we not then instruct the special committee to direct its studies toward realizing this end, which is the essential end? Would that be prejudging? I cannot see any way in which that would be prejudging. We ask that the provisions of the Covenant of the League of Nations and the provisions of the Charter of the United Nations be the basis for any solution to be found for Palestine, and nothing else.

Are we demanding anything exorbitant or anything which is irregular or out of order if we ask that the provisions of the Charter be applied and that they serve for the solution of the problem of Palestine? The Charter of the United Nations is the sole reason for linking us here altogether. Otherwise, we would not have the opportunity to meet each other in such a highly distinguished gathering, if there were no Charter. If we had not pledged loyalty to the Charter we would not have met. We have pledged loyalty and respect to all the provisions of the Charter, its principles and its purposes. Well, the terms of reference do not make any allusion to it.

I have heard some statements to the effect that if attempts of cooperation were made, the Jews and Arabs might live peacefully together. I say yes, we have made the attempts and we have put forward very definite principles to further such cooperation. The only thing which ought to be suppressed and done away with is the Zionist programme, which is continuous, unlimited immigration in order to have a Jewish majority in Palestine. Only then, would independence be granted. Well, how can we accept that the majority of the whole population of the country be made a minority, and that minority then be dominated by a foreign element. Certainly the Arabs would be upset to hear that, and they have every reason to resort to any means of self-defence; this we do not wish to happen. The Syrian Government is very unwilling to allow any disorder or disturbance to take place. But all of you who are living in democratic countries and under democratic parliamentary constitutions know to what extent the governmental power may influence and suppress the public feeling.

However there is a limit, after which the people would go beyond the power of their governments. We are afraid of that, and we are trying to draw the attention of the United Nations and the committee of inquiry to it so that they may have the principle of peace in the Near East, not only in Palestine but in the surrounding Arab world, as a basic object of their studies, and not allow anything which would cause disturbance in that country. At least for the sake of peace, if they do not care for justice and for the principles of self-determination as laid down in the Charter, let them consider peace at least sufficiently to make them careful in what they are going to do.

We say: "Let us try to have the Jews and Arabs of Palestine cooperate and establish good understanding among themselves". Well, if we suppose this is possible, I think it is more possible for the Jews to cooperate and create good understanding with the people of their own homes from which they have been displaced. Why do they not go back to the country which they have left, which is their country, and where they have their homes. It is easier to assimilate with people who speak the same language, and in whose country they are not intruders. For instance, if the Jews who left Poland would go back to Poland they would not be considered intruders, newcomers, outsiders, or invaders–they would be considered citizens of Poland. In Russia and in any other place it would be the same thing.

We understand that a great percentage of the Jews were

massacred in Eastern Europe. Well, the survivors, who are a small percentage under the ruling democracies of eastern Europe, could go back and take into their possession the properties of all the Jews who were there before, and each of them would be seven or eight times as rich as he used to be before. Further, he has for his protection, as has been claimed by various representatives, a full guarantee that democracy is prevailing. The representatives of those provinces even say that in their countries everything prevails, equality, democracy, full rights, liberty and fraternity. But, if it is so, why do the Jews hate to go back to those countries? Is it on a humanitarian basis? No, it is not on a humanitarian basis. It is a result of political ideas which are inspired in them by the Zionist leaders. They are pushing them on. If the Zionist leaders had not taken these steps, you would not find any Jew in Europe, America, or in any other place willing to go to Palestine.

Palestine is a tiny country. It is only ten thousand square miles, out of which only four thousand square miles can be cultivated, and the rest is made up of deserts, mountains and hills. It is inhabited now by approximately two million people. If we take the whole area of Palestine, we will find two hundred people on each square mile. Such a ratio does not exist in any state in America, though it does exist in some States of Europe, such as Belgium and Luxembourg. However, if we look at other sections we can find spacious areas where the Jews, if they really wish it, will be able to live peacefully, but not Palestine.

Palestine has already taken in six or seven hundred thousand Jews of the Jews who survived Hitler. Most of them are from among those who lived under Hitler's domination. Most of the Jews who are in Palestine now fled to that country from Germany while the latter was under Hitler's control. Let us suppose that Palestine ought to admit Jews. In fact it has taken more than it should. There is no room to take any more.

The Arab States are hospitable. Let me refer to what happened after the First World War. After the First World War, Syria and Lebanon took in two or three hundred thousand Armenian refugees who went there. They are still living there peacefully and quietly, and they are treated by the people with the greatest equality and given full rights. We now have Armenians as members of our parliaments, on an equal basis and an equal footing with the rest of the population. We received them, and they are welcome there. Why? Because they do not come with political views. They do not come to dominate; they do not come to exterminate the people, and take their homes and their right to sovereignty and self-determination.

Had the Jews gone to other parts of the Arab world, other than Palestine–because Palestine cannot hold any more–with the intention of finding a refuge there, they would have been treated with tolerance and indulgence. But this is not the case.

Although I have much to say about it, I am not going to discuss the administration in Palestine during the existing mandate. All the taxes and money collected there from the population were spent in establishing or promoting the Jewish national home. It is as if the Arabs of Palestine were asked to help in digging their graves with their own hands. I am sorry to say that.

SEVENTY-EIGHTH PLENARY MEETING
Held in the General Assembly Hall
Flushing Meadow, New York, Wednesday, 14 May 1947

II

Mr. Ben Gurion (Representative of the Jewish Agency): ... You are faced with a tragic problem, perhaps the tragic problem of our time and of many generations, of a people which was twice forcibly driven out of its country and which never acquiesces in its dispossession, and although it was its bitter destiny to wonder in exile for many centuries it always remained attached with all its heart and soul to its historic homeland. It is a unique fact in world history, but it is a real, living, incontestable fact. During your short visit in this country you have seen, I believe, some manifestations of this deep attachment. You have seen Jews from all parts of the World – the call of the homeland brought them here – who with passionate devotion to the soil of their ancestors are endeavouring to regenerate a people and a land. An unbroken tie between our people and our land has persisted through all these centuries in full force because of the fundamental historical facts: first, this country has remained largely desolate and waste while possessing great potentialities of development, given the need, skill, means and devotion for their realization. Second, Jewish homelessness and insecurity in the Diaspora, which is the underlying cause of all Jewish suffering and persecution. Jewish misery may vary from time to time, it may become more or less acute, but it never ceases. Jewish insecurity originates in three fundamental disabilities of Jews throughout the world; they are deprived of statehood, they are homeless and they are in a minority position everywhere. Unless and until these three disabilities are completely and lastingly remedied, there is no hope for the Jewish people, nor can there be justice in the world.

The homelessness and minority positions make the Jews always dependent on the mercy of others. The "others" may be good and may be bad, and the Jews may sometime be treated more or less decently, but they are never masters of their own destiny, they are entirely defenceless when the majority of people turn against them. What happened to our people in this war is merely a climax to uninterrupted persecution to which we have been subjected for centuries by almost all the Christian and Moslem peoples in the old world.

There were and there are many Jews who could not stand it, and they deserted us. They could not stand the massacres and expulsions, the humiliation and discrimination, and they gave it up in despair. But the Jewish people as a whole did not give way, did not despair or renounce its hope and faith in a better future, national as well as universal.

And here we are, not only we the Jews of Palestine, but the Jews throughout the world – the small remnant of European Jewry and Jews in other countries. We claim our rightful place under the sun as human beings and as a people, the same right as other human beings and peoples possess the right to security, freedom, equality, statehood and membership in the United Nations. No individual Jew can be really free, secure and equal anywhere in the world as long as the Jewish people as a people is not again rooted in its own country as an equal and independent nation.

An international undertaking was given to the Jewish people, some thirty years ago in the Balfour Declaration and in the Mandate for Palestine, to reconstitute our national home in our ancient homeland. This undertaking originated with the British people and the British Government. It was supported and confirmed by

52 nations and embodied in an international instrument known as the Mandate for Palestine. The Charter of the United Nations seeks to maintain "justice and respect for the obligations arising from treaties and other sources of international law." Is it too presumptuous on our part to expect that the United Nations will see that obligations to the Jewish people too are respected and faithfully carried out in the spirit and the letter? ...

The Balfour Declaration did not come out of the blue, British statesmen and thinkers had long taken a great interest in the national revival of the Jews in Palestine. In 1902, the British Government set up a Royal Commission to enquire into the question of aliens in England. Dr. Herzl, whose book on "The Jewish State as the only solution of the Jewish problem" was epoch-making in our history and who became the founder of modern Zionism, was invited by His Majesty's Government to give evidence before that Commission. His statement at the hearings that "the solution of the Jewish difficulty is the recognition of the Jews as a people and the finding by them of a legally-recognised home, to which Jews in those parts of the world where they are oppressed would naturally migrate" fell on fertile soil, and met with deep sympathy in the British Government. Palestine was then still part of the Ottoman Empire, so Mr. Joseph Chamberlain, then Secretary of State for the Colonies, offered Uganda to the Jews. While our people was deeply grateful for such an unprecedented offer, it was rejected by us, for the simple reason that it was not our historic homeland, it was not the Land of Israel. It was Russian and East European Jews who were mainly responsible for the rejection, in spite of the fact that the plight of our people in many countries and especially in Czarist Russia was at that time desperate. The British Government offered then the Zionists an alternative, a large area on the border of Palestine known as El Arish, which had been detached from Ottoman rule. This plan, too, came to nothing because of lack of water, and it was only the dissolution of the Ottoman Empire in the First World War which gave the British an opportunity to restore Palestine to the Jews.

The Balfour Declaration was not the first of its kind, just as this is not our first return. After the destruction of our first commonwealth by the Assyrians and Babylonians, the Persian King Cyrus the Great in the year 538 B.C. made the first "Balfour Declaration", as we are told in the Book of Ezra:

"In the first year of Cyrus King of Persia, that the word of the Lord by the mouth of Jeremiah might be accomplished, the Lord stirred up the spirit of Cyrus King of Persia, that he made a proclamation to the Jews throughout all his kingdom, and put it also in writing, saying, 'Thus saith Cyrus King of Persia: All the kingdoms of the earth hath the Lord, the God of heaven, given me; and He hath charged me to build Him a house in Jerusalem, which is in Judah. Whosoever there is among you of all His people – his God be with him – let him go up to Jerusalem, which is in Judah, and build the house of the Lord.'" The Iranian representative will excuse me for using the word "Persia" but that was the use in the Bible.

2,455 years after the Cyrus Declaration, another one was issued by Mr. Balfour on behalf of His Majesty's Government on November 2, 1917. I can safely assume that all of you are acquainted with the text of that document, but I must draw your attention to the first and last sentences, which are sometimes omitted when that document is quoted. The opening is this: "Dear Lord Rothschild, I have much pleasure in conveying to you on behalf of His Majesty's Government the following declaration of sympathy with Jewish Zionist aspirations, which has been submitted to and approved by the Cabinet." And the last sentence reads: "I should be grateful if you would bring this declaration to the knowledge of the Zionist Federation." The text of this declaration had been submitted to President Wilson and had been approved by him before its publication. The first people after Britain and America to associate itself with this declaration was Yugoslavia, or as it was then called, Serbia. Then came the confirmation of France, Italy, China and many others. Emir Feisal representing the Arabs at the Peace Conference on behalf of his father) the Sharif of Mecca, gave it his blessing.

"The field in which the Jewish National Home was to be established was understood at the time of the Balfour Declaration to be the whole of historic Palestine", stated the Royal Commission for Palestine of 1937. That is to say it included Transjordan. The meaning of the national home was at that time made abundantly clear by the authors of the Declaration. Mr. Lloyd George, who was Prime Minister at the time, testified: "The idea was, that a Jewish State was not to be set up immediately by the Peace Treaty it was…contemplated that…if the Jews had meanwhile responded to the opportunity and had become a definite majority of the inhabitants, then Palestine would thus become a Jewish Commonwealth." …

Now the question, the main and fundamental question arises: What should be the future regime of this country? It does not matter so much what name is given to the regime, whether you call it Mandate, International Trusteeship, Palestine State, National State, Arab State or Jewish State. Neither does it matter very much that the formal constitution would be. You have countries with good constitutions on paper and with bad governments in practice, and you have the reverse. Life does not follow paper constitutions.

I will give you an example of a name which can cover different purposes: the term or name "bi-national state". I know at least two projects for a national state in Palestine which are diametrically opposed to each other. One based on the very denial of Zionism and the National Home whereas the other is a full-blooded Zionist scheme.

The anti-Zionist bi-national state is the White Paper of Mr. Malcolm Macdonald, who claims that his policy envisages neither a Jewish nor an Arab State, but a bi-national one. Although the Jews will form one third of the population, the state will not be Arab, but will be shared by both peoples, and shared in such a way that the essential interests of each community are safeguarded. It even promises to protect the special position of the Jewish National Home in Palestine. This is a bi-national state which prohibits Jewish immigration, condemns Jews to remain a permanent minority and perpetuates the homelessness of the Jewish people.

And there is another proposal for a bi-national state advanced by [an] important labour left-wing group in Zionism, the Labour party "Hashomer Hatzair". It is a project to settle from two to three million Jews in Palestine in the next 25 years. For that period Palestine would be placed, according to that plan, under the administration of a special Development Authority, the specific objective of which would be:

(i) to promote the settlement in Palestine of
at least 2 to 3 million Jews during the next

20 or 25 years by developing the economic possibilities of the country.

(ii) to raise the standard of living and education of the Palestinian Arabs to approximately the present Jewish level during the same period.

(iii) To promote and actively encourage Jewish cooperation as well as to encourage the gradual development of self-governing institutions, local and national, on bi-national lines, until the stage of full independence within the framework of a bi-national constitution is reached.

To achieve this, Palestine would be placed under a Permanent Supervisory Commission of the three Great Powers and this Commission would be responsible for selecting an administration fitted to fulfill the afore-mentioned tasks. A development Board is to be instituted by that government in which Jews and Arabs will participate in equal numbers.

When independence had been achieved after some twenty to twenty-five years, the Permanent Supervisory Commission would continue to execute some powers of general supervision until the United Nations decided that the new constitution was working well and that Palestine was ready for membership of the United Nations.

Jews and Arabs would be organised in two national, autonomous communities; when Palestine became independent, it would be constituted as a federation of these two communities. The Central Government would consist of four members, two Arabs and two Jews, elected by a State Assembly, composed of the two

National Councils of the Jewish and Arab communities and of the State Council with half Jews and half Arabs.

You can easily see that, although these are both called bi-national state plans, they mean in reality two contradictory things. The question of the future regime in Palestine is really not so much a question of legal, constitutional arrangements, but a more fundamental question of the desired future structure of the country, the make-up, size and composition of the population and the nature of the development of its resources. The most crucial question is immigration. Here you are faced with two possible lines of action: the anti-Zionist line, which is that the constitution of the country should preserve the status quo, freeze the size and the growth of the present population, arrest the development of agriculture and industry, stop immigration and turn Jews into a statutory minority.

And there is another line – the Zionist line – that the regime of the country should be designed to realise the maximum development of all the potentialities of Palestine; to cultivate as many millions of dunums [dunum = 0.2471 acre] as possible out of the 18 million dunums which are at present uncultivated; to irrigate instead of 400,000 dunums as at present, at least 4,000,000 dunums; to increase the size of the population to three or four millions and afford full opportunities for the Jewish people to rehabilitate themselves, while raising the standard of the Arabs to the same level, and in this way to create a living example for the Whole Middle East, where Jews and Arabs will cooperate and work together as free and equal partners.

I venture to submit that the second line was envisaged and adopted by the statesmen – British, Arabs and Jews

– at the end of the first world war when a general desire for a new social order and new international relations stirred humanity. It was felt that the time had come to redress the ancient wrong committed against the Jewish nation and to give it a chance to restore its ancient commonwealth.

It was part of a larger arrangement which gave the Arabs their national freedom after many centuries of Turkish oppression. It is wrong to regard the problem of Jewish-Arab relations only in the framework of this little country. The statesmen who were responsible for the Balfour Declaration did not envisage merely the restoration of the Jewish nation alone. At the same time they provided for the liberation of the Arab people and they achieved this on a much larger scale and in a more effective way. The Arabs gained their freedom in an area of 1,250,000 square miles, 125 times as large as the area of Western Palestine with a population of some 15 to 16 million Arabs – about the number of Jews living then in the world.

This was the real two-fold arrangement made with the Arabs and the Jews. The freedom of the Arab people in their countries – the restoration of Palestine to the Jewish people. ...

One may rightly ask: Why is it that a million Arabs can be safely left in a Jewish State and why should not a million Jews be left in an Arab State? If the Jews and the Arabs who are in Palestine were all the Jews and all the Arabs that exist in the world, this would be a very logical and conclusive argument. There would then be no reason whatsoever why one should prefer an Arab to a Jew or a Jew to an Arab, and only numbers would count. But one cannot ignore the fact that both communities living in Palestine are merely fragments of larger communities living outside, and both of them belong to these larger units and their fates are inextricably bound up with the larger units. By depriving the Jews in Palestine of a national home, by preventing them from becoming a majority and attaining statehood, you are depriving not only 600,000 Jews who are here, but also the millions of Jews who are still left in the world, of independence and statehood. ... In depriving the million Arabs of the same prospect, you do not affect the status of the Arab race at all. An Arab minority in a Jewish State would mean that only a certain number of individual Arabs would not enjoy the privilege of Arab statehood, but it would in no way diminish the independence and position of the free Arab race. The Arab minority in Palestine, being surrounded by Arab States, would remain safe in national association with their race. ...

SPECIAL COMMITTEE ON PALESTINE
VERBATIM RECORD OF THE SIXTEENTH MEETING (PUBLIC)
Held at the Y.M.C.A. Building
Jerusalem, Palestine
Friday, 4 July 1947

Mr. BEN GURION (Representative of the Jewish Agency): ...We have no conflict with the Arabs on our side. As far as this country and the Arabs are concerned, what we say is that we were dispossessed from our country, although it was a considerable time ago. But we did not give it up. It is our home. We admit that all those who are living in this country have the same right to it, just as we. We do not say, as in the case of other dispossessed people, that the people who are there ought to be removed. There was such a view held by the Labour Party, adopted only two years ago by the British Labour Party, just before the election, that in order to make more room for Jews the Arabs should be encouraged to transfer to other countries. We did not accept it even then; we did not approve of it. We do not claim that any Arab ought to be removed. Therefore, we have no conflict, as far as we are concerned, with the Arabs. They deny our right to be in our home. If you call this a conflict, then there is a conflict, but it is not a conflict on our side.

...

[W]e say that the original intention and the need, and what in our conviction is just, should be decided upon by the United Nations, and a Jewish State should be established. There are two parts in the establishment of a state: one is the material part, which is the most essential; the other is the legal part, the purely formal one, which is also of great importance.

I will say a word about the material establishment, because the whole difficulty of the problem here is that you have a people, you have a country, and their right to the country was acknowledged, but the people do not happen to be there yet. They were dispossessed, and they have to come back. So, the first thing is the material establishment of the state, which means that plans based on our experience and on achievements, examined and approved by experts, economic, irrigation, agricultural, industrial experts, and so on – should be examined by the Committee and the United Nations to see how they can be carried out; and that a million Jews would be resettled in their country.

In our view it is not only possible, but it is possible to do so by good will. It is possible to do it in a very short time. This is the material establishment of a national home for the Jewish State. This may take some time. In the meantime, it will be supervised by the highest authority of the United Nations. The fact that the Mandatory itself referred it to the United Nations implies a certain recognition that this is the place where it has to be judged and decided, although the Mandatory did not undertake formally to carry it out. But there is an indication that this is the place where it should be decided.

Assuming that on the recommendations of your Committee the United Nations approves of that plan, the material establishment, it means the settlement of the first million Jews – I say a million, it may be 900,000 or it may be 1,100,000, to state a round figure – in the shortest possible time. Even the shortest possible time may and must take more time. I am unable to say how long it will take. I think no one is able to say that, because there are always in human affairs unforeseen things which may happen. But it should not take longer, as far as we can judge now – it must not take longer than a few years. Not necessarily longer than a few years. Then, in the meantime, a committee or any instrument which the United Nations will decide on, will supervise.

This plan means two things: bringing in a large number of Jews, and developing the Arab parts of the country. Because we cannot – not only because we are philanthropists – we cannot irrigate the country as a whole – and the basis of our plan is, first of all, irrigation. You cannot irrigate only the Jewish part of the land. You must irrigate all parts of the land. And we must give irrigation to the Arabs. We must give roads to the Arabs. We must give better buildings and better schools. And it implies raising the standard of living of the Arabs to the same level, as possible, as the Jewish.

These are the two essential features of our plan of development: a large Jewish settlement; a considerable raising of Arab standards. When this plan is approved by you and by the United Nations, then the Jewish Agency can be charged to carry it out, not only because it is responsible but because it is able to do it. We will be able to do it. It is our baby. If the Arabs are willing to take part, we will welcome them to take part in it. It will be under the highest supervision of the United Nations.

When a considerable part of the plan is carried out, because you must not wait until the end of it − a considerable portion of that large-scale plan of immigration, settlement and improvement of conditions of Arabs is carried out, then the United Nations will decide there is no more need for supervision and the independent state of Palestine can be established. And we can envisage a state in Palestine only on absolutely Democratic lines, where every citizen in the country is an equal citizen. By the way, I want to express what we mean by a Jewish state. We mean by a Jewish State simply a state where the majority of the people are Jews, not a state where a Jew has, in any way, any privilege, more than anyone else.

I want to mention on this occasion that during our last talks with the Government in London, when certain proposals were made for a settlement − which, unfortunately, we could not consider − we were offered that Jews should have more rights than others. And certain examples were given us of certain British colonies, in Ceylon and other places. And we declared emphatically to the Government that we will not accept, we will fight any privilege accorded to a Jew because he is a Jew. What we want to have is more Jews in Palestine but not more privileges for the Jews. A Jewish state means a state based on absolute equality of all her citizens and on democracy. When the United Nations will see that the main purpose for which this country is destined, to solve the Jewish problem, that the main thing has been done and that the time is ripe to undertake administration of the Government itself – then the second phase, the legal, the formal establishment of a state will be reached. In either it will take two years, three years, I cannot say, but in that transition period it will be in the charge of the United Nations. That is all we envisage here.

CHAIRMAN [Emil Sandström, Sweden]: If I sum up correctly what you have said, you mean that it would be an administration of the country under supervision by the United Nations?

Mr. BEN GURION: Yes, the Jewish Agency –

CHAIRMAN: But is that not a continuation of the Mandate in another form?

Mr. BEN GURION: No, it is not. Because the Mandate means – you will see the first article of the Mandate begins: "That the Mandatory shall have full power of legislation and of administration...save as they may be limited by the terms of this Mandate." This had to be done because at the beginning there was only a very small Jewish community of some 60,000 and they could not foresee how long it would take to reach the consummation of the purpose of the Mandate. We are now in a different phase. There is only a very short interval between the decision to have a Jewish state and the material and legal consummation of a state.

CHAIRMAN: Of course, when I asked whether it is not a continuation of the Mandate, that was a contradiction, as there will be no Mandatory. It will be a direct administration by the United Nations. But do you think there is an advantage in such a situation?

Mr. BEN GURION: There is, because, first of all, there will be a clear-cut, equivocal decision that Palestine is becoming a Jewish state. The fact – and this has been admitted by many – the fact that this was not quite clear in the Mandate has led to contradictions. But the first thing is that there will be a clear-cut decision. Then the interval will be very short. Therefore, although you can say what is the difference if you call it a Mandate or if you call it supervision – the difference is that it is for a very short time, you know exactly where you are going, and you know what is going to happen in a few years.

...

Sir Abdur RAHMAN (India): Do I understand correctly that you want a Jewish state to be established, to be forced on the country by the arms of the United Nations?

CHAIRMAN: I was just going to put a similar question. I understand this one hundred per cent Jewish solution of the Palestine question and a complete dismissal of the Arab claim to the country. I suppose you agree with me that it is.

Mr. BEN GURION: I will tell you – first of all, I think I ought to answer the question of Sir Abdur Rahman.

CHAIRMAN: I will come to that, but at a later stage.

What do you think will be the Arab reaction to such a solution?

Mr. BEN GURION: Well, I will answer both questions. I will answer first the question I was asked by Sir Abdur Rahman.

CHAIRMAN: I am coming to the same question that Sir Abdur Rahman asked after you answer this one. What do you think will be the reaction?

Mr. BEN GURION: Do you want me to answer your question first and then the question of Sir Abdur Rahman?

CHAIRMAN: Yes, sir.

Mr. BEN GURION: Well, you asked me a question which I am afraid is not for me to answer. I am sorry that you have no Arab representatives here, because this question can be really authoritatively answered by them. I cannot say. I would not presume to tell you what may or may not be the Arab reactions because, as far as I know, there may be different reactions of different people and I know there are different attitudes. I happen to know this.

CHAIRMAN: Now I come to the question of Sir Abdur Rahman.

Sir ABDUR RAHMAN (India): In connection with your own question, Mr. Chairman, would it not mean a war between the Jews and the Arabs? Let us put it straight. Would it not mean an absolutely bloody war between the Jews and the Arabs?

Mr. BEN GURION: Do you want me to answer this question now?

CHAIRMAN: Yes, please.

Mr. BEN GURION: I will answer the question as it was put to me first and as it is put to me now.

Sir Abdur RAHMAN (India): They are two different questions.

Mr. BEN GURION: I want to answer both questions. The first question is whether we want the United Nations to force upon the Arabs a Jewish state or Jewish immigration. This was the question.

Sir Abdur RAHMAN (India): The Chairman wants the second question to be answered first.

Mr. BEN GURION: Do you want me to answer the second question?

CHAIRMAN: I do not want to press my question. What I wanted to know was whether one could assume that there will be a violent Arab reaction. Then you have to answer the question which Sir Abdur Rahman put.

Mr. BEN GURION: Yes. The supposition is that no armed forces are loosed against anybody. First of all, I want to say that the fact implied in that question that at present armed forces are not being used is not quite correct. The present position is that armed forces are being used against us. Armed forces are being used against Jews that are coming into the country. But for the armed forces of the British Navy, the Jews who are still suffering in camps would be here. Because it is only the armed forces that have prevented them from coming.

Before I answer the question, I will ask this question: Are you for using forces of the United Nations or of a

Mandatory to prevent Jews, by force, from coming back to their country, a thing which is happening now?

CHAIRMAN: We will not answer that question. I have the answer to our question.

Mr. BEN GURION: I am not asking you a question; I am not asking you to answer.

CHAIRMAN: You are answering my question.

Mr. BEN GURION: I have to answer. I said that the facts are that at present force is being used against us for two purposes: for preventing us from coming here – because, without force, I want Sir Abdur Rahman to know these Jews would not have been prevented from coming back; and secondly, force is used to enforce the racial discrimination against Jews.

Sir ABDUR RAHMAN (India): That is not the answer to the question. It is going absolutely beyond it. If he would only concentrate on the answer to the question put to him, it would be better, because when he says force is being used, the same force is being used against the Arabs, and the same force is being used against anybody who contravenes the law. If I contravene the law, the same force would be used against me today.

Mr. BEN GURION: I did not finish my answer.

Sir Abdur RAHMAN (India): You are going beyond it. You will not finish for two months if you go on in that way. I do not mind if we take two months or two years. Let me lead the questioning. You say you have not finished your answer?

Mr. BEN GURION: Yes. I say that the fact is, first, that force is being used against people exercising their rights. Our right is to come back. To prevent this, force is being used.

If the United Nations will give a decision in justice and equity that the Jews have a right to come back to their country, then I believe it will be their duty, if necessary, to enforce it. I do not know how much force will be necessary, but you have the same problem everywhere in the world. The main question is not whether to use force or not; the main question is whether a thing is right or wrong. That is what the United Nations have to decide: Is it right or is it wrong? If it is wrong, then it is for the United Nations to stop every Jew from coming into the country, and perhaps, as some people here want, to send away those who are here. Such a thing has happened to us. So, this is the question: if the United Nations will say this is right, then they will do everything to enforce that right, the same as they are doing to enforce right everywhere else in the world. It is not a special question applied to us.

CHAIRMAN: The object of this transitory period of administration, in order to get in the immigrants and to enforce that policy, implies, I suppose, the object of coming to a state where you could use afterwards democratic means to govern the country?

Mr. BEN GURION: Yes. When the country has reached a stage when the main object for which this country has to serve can be fulfilled, then you do not need any foreign intervention any more.

CHAIRMAN: The object is to create the conditions for a democratic rule of the country?

Mr. BEN GURION: Yes, sir.

CHAIRMAN: Now, let us return to the Arab claim. You know well the Arab claim and the basis for it?

Mr. BEN GURION: Yes.

CHAIRMAN: It can be expressed very shortly. It is a claim based on the possession of the land for a considerable period of and the right of self-government of the people on the land. What is your answer to this claim?

Mr. BEN GURION: My answer to that claim is the answer which was given not only by us but by human conscience almost in the whole world. The same claim was made almost twenty-five years ago. The reply was that you cannot judge this country which has a special history and special conditions which cannot be found anywhere else, and the relations of the Jews of this country cannot be judged by a rule applied to other countries not having the same unique conditions. Really, it is a unique case. You have first of all the people who were here a very, very long time ago; you know that.

I can give you the Arab case. I understand the Arab case and I fully realize it. It is very simple. They state they do not care what happened, and nobody ought to care what happened fifteen hundred or two thousand years ago. We are here. We are not here from yesterday; we were here for centuries. We are the majority, and we have a right to self-determination. We will decide, just as the people in the United States or the people in Canada, whether to allow or not to allow immigrants. The fact that Jews were here some two thousand years ago is the same as the Roman legions having been in

England some two thousand years ago, or when Arabs were in Spain fourteen or so many centuries ago. That is their claim. It is simple.

Not one but many nations in the world did not accept that claim because they were faced with a unique case which is not as simple as that. You cannot compare it with Spain and the Arabs. Can you find a single Arab in the world who cares to go back to Spain? Can you find a single Arab in the world who will spend a penny for Spain? Can you find a single Arab in the world who dreams of Spain? What has he to do with Spain? He has his own country.

Many kinds of people come from many countries, but here you have a unique case without any parallel in history. Here is a people who for many centuries were dreaming of this country. They might have found a country anywhere else, but no, and they never gave up their claim. It is unique. Also, the case of Palestine is unique. It is not the same. We did not say it alone, but the entire civilized world said that while the Arabs were liberated in various territories there was room for the Jews in Palestine. The Jews are connected with the country. We recognize their connection. They are coming back. They have a right to come back. They put only one limitation. We, ourselves, would have put this limitation if it had not been put by others: not to displace the population right here. I do not know if I have to go into that again. That was the decision. What happened? Nothing happened. Did it prove the Jews do not need a home? Did it prove that Jews cannot build? Was it proven that we can come in only by displacing Arabs? Everything that happened since that world decision strengthened that decision. The need of the Jews, their ability to come back, and their not displacing (I do not want to bring in the point that we are benefiting anyone – we are, but not because of that), these three things were proven even more than they were known twenty-five years ago.

Now, I return to the question: what reason have you, not you the Commission, but what reason has world conscience to reverse that decision? There is only one reason that the people here say "No, [we] will not let those Jews come back." The same thing happened in many countries. In certain countries the Government submitted that, and I do not want to mention the names of those countries. There are Jews who were dispossessed by Hitler. I do not speak of Germany, but countries that suffered from Hitler. When the Jews were dispossessed, very few, because the majority were murdered, came back and claimed their possessions. They did not get them back for the simple reason that the countries were occupied and did not want to give them back. That was the only reason. But this case is not similar to that because then the Jews had three or four rooms and, in the meantime, somebody else occupied all the three rooms.

Here we have a case where there is a large building and three rooms are occupied, eleven rooms are not occupied, and we say, "Stay in your three rooms, we are going to occupy the other eight unoccupied rooms." He says, "No we don't want it. Stay out." The world has said "No", and we say there is no reason why you should reverse that decision because justice and necessity are the same, if not stronger. There is no reason whatsoever. The only reason is that those who undertook to do it failed to do it.

CHAIRMAN: You think the fact that a claim to a country has not been given up is so essential?

Mr. BEN GURION: Our claim?

CHAIRMAN: Yes.

Mr. BEN GURION: It is very. Of course, if we are invaders, then we have no right.

CHAIRMAN: And you do not think that a thousand year's possession is enough to oust the claim?

Mr. BEN GURION: Sir, I do not lay down general rules. I say on this occasion, under this historic and geographic position, no it is not, for the reasons which I gave in my address. It is not a question of the Arab race; they are fully liberated. It is not a question of the Arab individuals who are here; they are not suffering. Our claim stands; we did not give it up.

...

CHAIRMAN: There is one argument in the Arab case to which I want an answer. They say this decision of the League of Nations is all right, but nobody can dispose of our country without our consent. What do you answer to that?

Mr. BEN GURION: The answer is this is our country, including the Arabs who are in it. This country is the country of the Jewish people and of all the other inhabitants. This is our answer.

SPECIAL COMMITTEE ON PALESTINE
VERBATIM RECORD OF THE NINETEENTH MEETING (PUBLIC)
Held at the Y.M.C.A. Building
Jerusalem, Palestine
Monday, 7 July 1947

Sir Abdur RAHMAN (India): Is it possible for you to imagine that any country in the world – Canada, Australia, the United States of America, South Africa or England – will permit Jewish immigration in unlimited numbers if they are exposed to the risk of being outnumbered?

Mr. BEN GURION: I do not feel any need to imagine such a thing. If you mean to ask why we want to come to Palestine, I have told you it is because we are coming back to our country. But I do not know why you want me to imagine such a thing could happen except in our country. Of course we do not imagine, we could not imagine such a thing. On the contrary, I told you in my opening speech that we were offered space in another country, in Africa: we refused it on that account, because we did not consider it our country.

Sir Abdur RAHMAN (India): Do you imagine the friendship between the Jews and the Arabs will increase if unlimited immigration is permitted in Palestine?

Mr. BEN GURION: I imagine that when the Jews are re-established as an independent nation they will establish good relations between themselves and their neighbours. Without it, no. There will be trouble with the Arabs who think they could do with the Jews what the Europeans did with them.

Sir Abdur RAHMAN (India): Have the relations between Arabs and Jews been very strained since the Mandate?

Mr. BEN GURION: As I said, relations between individual Jews and individual Arabs were often very good – in Turkish times, and they are very good now, but political relations between Arab communities and

Jewish communities are not so good, and this is because they have been brought into opposition.

Sir Abdur RAHMAN (India): Who was in possession and occupation of Palestine as it is known today before the Israelites?

Mr. BEN GURION: There were a large number of people who came here there are many names.

CHAIRMAN: Before whom?

Sir Abdur RAHMAN (India): Before the Israelites.

Mr. BEN GURION: The names are supplied in our Bible.

Sir Abdur RAHMAN (India): All of them have died out?

Mr. BEN GURION: Yes, all of them.

Six Abdur RAHMAN (India): All of them and their descendants have died.

Mr. BEN GURION: Yes, they disappeared.

Sir Abdur RAHMAN (India): And the fellaheen [Arab peasant farmers] who exist in Palestine today, are they descendants?

Mr. BEN GURION: I do not think so.

...

Sir Abdur RAHMAN (India): When did the Jews leave Palestine?

Mr. BEN GURION: They never left it.

Sir Abdur RAHMAN (India): They have always been here?

Mr. BEN GURION: Yes, except in the period of the Crusades, when all Jews were entirely exterminated.

Sir Abdur RAHMAN (India): When was that?

Mr. BEN GURION: You know it was the 10th, 11th and 12th centuries.
...

Mr. ENTEZAM (Iran) (Interpretation from French): ... As I see it, Mr. Ben Gurion admits to only one solution, and that is an independent state of Palestine. It is quite evident that on that point Mr. Ben Gurion and the Arabs are in full agreement. Both want an independent state, and both want a democratic state. I insist on the words "democracy" and democratic state" because, in the first place, it is a fashionable and popular expression at present, and also because it means rule by the majority. The only difference between the Arabs and the Jewish people on this point is that the Arabs say "establish that independent state now"; whereas the Jewish people say "don't do it now, but wait until we have a majority in the country."

If we admit that Palestine is a special case and might need special treatment, can we at the same time accept under the question of delay the principle of self-determination? It seems to me that it is difficult to admit at the same time that you must delay until an independent state is established and also admit the principle of self-determination. This is the question I have.

Mr. BEN GURION: ... When there is an over-riding right which may displace that right of self-determination no country will recognize – neither Persia nor France – the right of self-determination, let us say, of one of their dependents to be independent. There are certain rights of self-determination, and when I say the right of the Jew to come back to his country and the right of our people to be here as equal partners in the world family, it is an over-riding right which applies to Palestine, and therefore no regime – not only an Arab State – should be created – even no trusteeship, no mandate should be created – which will make that right impossible of realisation. This is why we oppose it. It is not a matter of time only, but given sufficient framework, it can be safeguarded only if there is independence and the Jews are in the majority. Then the Jew will be able to come back if he is persecuted. I am not naming any country – let us say Patagonia – but if he is in danger of being murdered or persecuted there he will be able to come back if there is a place for him because the majority will see to it. And the Jewish people as a whole – not every Jew – will enjoy the same status as any other people. This is the crucial point, and not the matter of time.

SPECIAL COMMITTEE ON PALESTINE
VERBATIM RECORD OF THE TWENTY-FIRST MEETING (PUBLIC)
Held at the Y.M.C.A. Building
Jerusalem, Palestine
Tuesday, 8 July 1947

III

Dr. WEIZMANN: I should like to begin my statement — and I do so from the bottom of my heart — by expressing in the presence of you gentlemen and of the public sitting here my sincerest gratitude to the Mandatory Power, to Great Britain, for having inaugurated this policy and for having, throughout many years, tried to go along with us in the implementation of this policy. There is no question, whatever may be the position today, that if we see today a great and interesting and thriving community in Palestine, it would not have been possible without first of all the conquest of Palestine by the British Army and the rule of Great Britain in this country. And that is a sincere tribute of gratitude, whatever else may have happened since. I consider that what is going on now — the deterioration of the relations between us and Great Britain, which, together with a great many Jews, I deplore, is merely a temporary thing which, in the light of the historic perspective in the past, is an unpleasant intermezzo.

Although the initiative of the Balfour Declaration came primarily from Great Britain, it is common knowledge that Great Britain had at the time the support of the Allied and associated Powers of France, of Italy, and, above all, of the United States of America; and subsequently the Mandate and the Balfour Declaration and the whole of the Palestinian Regime were, so to speak, a child of the League of Nations, and Great Britain was a trustee on behalf of the League. It had to account for its actions annually to the Permanent Mandates Commission of the League. The Permanent Mandates Commission was to draw up an annual report, and this report was to be submitted to the League

Assembly, which took the opportunity of expressing its approval or disapproval, wholly or partially, of the stewardship of the British Administration in Palestine. It went on like that for almost a quarter of a century, until the year 1939, until the publication of the White Paper which interrupted this work and which broke our existing relationship with the British Government, with the Administration of Palestine, very much to the regret of all the well-wishers of Palestine. ...

The Mandate, in my humble opinion, had two main purposes, and perhaps I will be permitted before I enter upon the subject to say a word about the motives which have moved Great Britain, and perhaps some other friends of both Great Britain and of the Jewish people, at that time to issue the Balfour Declaration. I know that a great deal of if I may be permitted, for lack of a better parliamentary expression, to use the word – nonsense is being spoken about it, and perhaps this is the time and the place to put it right, at any rate on behalf of one who, I think, was closely connected for many years with this period of Jewish and international history. Like every human deed, the Balfour Declaration had two main motives. There was no question but that it had an ideal motive. The statesmen of that time, Mr. Balfour and Mr. Lloyd George, amongst them, primarily wanted to manifest a certain amount of restitution to the Jewish people for the contribution which the Jews have made in these thousands of years to the civilisation of mankind, which, you know, is common knowledge. Mr. Lloyd George and Mr. Balfour were deeply religious men and knew the Bible, knew the value of the Bible and the effect the Bible had on the character and on the life of the British nation, and they could not help and were only too glad to connect this influence with the others of the Bible or with the nation in the midst of whom the Bible was born. I remember very well in the first talk which I had with Mr. Lloyd George – that was long before there was any talk of a Declaration or similar action – that he said, in a way half-jokingly and half-seriously – "You talk to me about Palestine. That is the only geography which I know, and I am acquainted with the geography of Palestine almost better than with the geography of the present Front. He was proud to be with this work, and there was no doubt an underlying ideal motive which moved the statesmen of that time – primarily the two foremost statesmen – to issue this Declaration.

There was, as I said, another set of motives and they were utilitarian; not utilitarian in a gross or purely materialistic sense, as I am going to explain in a moment. We were – I mean the British people and those who were associated with the British, and I was associated with the British nation and proud to be so all engaged in a war of life and death, which meant the existence or non-existence of the Commonwealth of Great Britain. A great deal depended upon America. In America there was a powerful Jewish community which was at that time, for some reason or other – I do not agree with this reason, but it was more or less current opinion in Great Britain at that time – either very neutral or inclined to be pro-German, some of them, the powerful German Jews, or the Jews of German ancestry. It was thought that by this act of restitution – at any rate a form of declaration – this might swing the opinion of a powerful group of American Jewry.

There was also another group – the Zionist group – which was never pro-German. It was always anxious to see British victory. But we wanted to have a united Jewish community of America standing behind the great war effort and behind President Wilson, who was carefully preparing his nation for entry into the war, for taking upon themselves a great ordeal, and it was thought that the Balfour Declaration might help to swing the opinion of this community. I believe it had some effect, and I believe that in that respect it has fulfilled the purpose which was intended of that time. There was also another community at that time which played a great part in the war – another Jewish community – and that was the Russian Jewish Community. It was, you remember, before Russia was divided and before Poland was re-established, and the Russian-Jewish Community was the largest in the world. It was six million strong and also the opinion of the Russian-Jewish Community was of considerable value in that constellation of circumstances. There were two purposes: one was purely idealistic, and the other partly utilitarian, in the sense in which I have tried to describe. I hope I may be forgiven for having dwelt on it at such length, but I thought now is the time, and I am advanced in years and I may not have the opportunity of clearing it up again, so I am taking the opportunity now of resubmitting it to you, gentlemen.

The nations of the world realized, particularly the British, Americans, French and Italians, that a great deal of the trouble, worry and persecution which has beset the Jews throughout their history is due to the abnormal position of the Jews in the world. What is the abnormal position of the Jews in the world? What is it characterized by? It is characterized by one thing: I think this word from what I can see from reports, has been used here quite often. I used this word for the first time in speaking before the Royal Commission. It is the "homelessness" of the Jewish people. To that I must add a comment. I do not mean the "homelessness" of individual Jews. There are groups of Jews in the world who have very comfortable homes – the American

Jews, the Jews in a great many of the Western and Northwestern countries, the Jews in Sweden, Denmark, France, and also there was in Germany — but as a collectivity, as an ethnic group, they are homeless. They are and they are not. They are a people and they lack the props of a people. They are a disembodied ghost. There they are with a great many typical characteristics, many strong characteristics which have not disappeared throughout centuries, thousands of years of martyrdom and wandering, and at the same time they lack the props which characterize every nation. We ask today: "What are Poles? What are French? What are Swiss?" When that is asked everyone points to a country, to certain institutions, to parliamentary institutions, and the man in the street will know exactly what it is. He has a passport. If you ask what a Jew is, well, he is a man who has to offer a long explanation for his existence. And, any person who has to offer an explanation as to what he is is always suspect, and from suspicion there is only one step to hatred or contempt. I am trying to put it as lightly as I can. I do not want to describe it as the tragedy which it really is. This has rendered the position of the Jews in the world abnormal and, as a very logical consequence of this abnormal position, their relation to the outside world is abnormal.

Palestine is in the process of upbuilding, having a thriving community here, yet even today there are Jews, I do not know how many, but quite a few who would deny (a) that there are Jews; (b) that they are Jews; (c) that there is Palestine; (d) that it is necessary to have Palestine. All that confuses the Gentile mind; which does not understand. And, if you do not understand somebody, you begin to suspect him. And, if you begin to suspect him, there is only one step left from suspicion to hatred. It was thought that this position must be remedied by normalizing the position of the Jews and by rendering them as normal as anybody else, and giving them those props and those material attributes which they lack. Hence the attempt and ardent desire of a great part of Jewry to build up a normal life of their own. And where could we do it except in this country?

I think I have, it is my duty, although I never thought it should be necessary, to try to explain "Why Palestine?" Why not Kamchatka, Alaska, Mexico, or Texas? There are a great many empty countries. Why should the Jews choose a country which has a population that does not want to receive you in a particularly friendly way; a small country; a country which has been neglected and derelict for centuries. It seems unusual on the part of a practical and shrewd people like the Jews to sink their effort, their sweat and blood, their substance into the sands, rocks and marshes of Palestine. Well, I could, if I wished to be facetious, say it is not our responsibility – not the responsibility of the Jews who sit here – it is the responsibility of Moses, who acted from divine inspiration. He might have brought us to the United States, and instead of the Jordan we might have had the Mississippi. It would have been an easier task. But, he has chosen to stop here. We are an ancient people with an old history, and you cannot deny your history and begin afresh. And the proof of what I am saying, which may again, perhaps, be too abstract, is the following: Almost parallel, simultaneously with the colonization of Palestine began another project of colonization in another part of the world far removed from here, nearer to a great many countries from which some of the distinguished representatives who sit here come from, that is the colonization in the Argentine. The colonization of Jews in the Argentine began, as I say, almost simultaneously with the attempt to colonize Palestine. Now, compare these two countries: Argentina is a vast country with virgin soil which had a benevolent government. There was no opposition. On the contrary, the government was anxious that the Jews should come in – at any rate then, I do not know what it is now. Usually this anxiety does not last too long – but there it was, and the Jews went to the Argentine. They went there under the guidance of a powerful committee, which was endowed with a great many funds, something to the amount of 10 million pounds, gold pounds. At that time it meant more than probably 50 or 75 millions now. They began their work under the best possible auspices. Today, the colonization of Argentina represents a few Jewish settlements. They are quite good, and they are decent people who work hard on the soil, but it is just a few Jewish villages. The younger generation of many of the Jewish settlements is drifting gradually to Buenos Aires where they become lawyers and doctors, the usual process which we know is the economic and social development of a Jewish community surrounded by a majority of non-Jews.

We began in this country at the same time. You have seen it. You have seen it now. Now, in a great many parts it looks attractive. It is covered with trees and grass. But I remember when I first came in 1908 and then in 1918 when I travelled with General Allenby, a great Commander-in-chief who conquered Palestine – I travelled with him from Ramallah, from Tel-Aviv to Jerusalem, and we travelled through a derelict, barren country. There was not much green, and he turned to me and said: "I thought you were a reasonable fellow. Do you really think anybody will come and settle in this country?" All I could say to Allenby, for whom I had a profound respect, was "well, General, let us wait another 20 years and perhaps we will be granted the opportunity of meeting again and we might rediscuss the subject." We did meet again, and we did rediscuss the subject, and he did change his mind, and he did announce the change publicly. Now, this progress is due to the fact that it is Palestine. Palestine, for reasons which I need not labor, releases energies, activities in the Jewish people which are not released anywhere else. As soon as a Jew comes into contact with this country he begins to feel as if he has returned. I shall not say that every Jew feels it. I am not going to say that he feels it at once. But these are sentiments which grow, which grew in everyone of us, and the rocks, marshes, and sands of Palestine become a precious possession into which we pour our sweat, blood, effort and ingenuity in order to make it what it is.

I gave some of the reasons for the Balfour Declaration in 1917. They were, as I said, ideal, and they were what is called "utilitarian." They also came as a result of a conception that the position of the Jew would be altered and his suffering allayed if he had a place to go to. And, if these reasons were valid in 1918, they a fortiori are one thousand times more valid today. I am afraid that the reasons which prompted us to make a prognosis of the Jewish problem in the years 1904, 1905, and 1906, for which we were looked upon as dreamers and star-gazers who were trying to get something impossible – all these prognoses as to what was going to happen to the Jews, unfortunately more than came true. There are six million Jews dead in Europe, and hundreds of thousands of Jews are languishing today either in Displaced Person camps or in countries where they are not wanted. It is proof that the situation demands speedy remedy. I say emphatically, gentlemen, speedy remedy. I took upon myself the liberty, perhaps it appears somewhat formal, last year to warn the Anglo-American Commission that time is of the essence. I am old enough to issue that warning again. Time is of the essence. We have lost so much blood, we cannot afford to lose any more. For us it is a question of survival: it brooks no delay. The position of Jewry today in the world is sombre. In Palestine it is somewhat different, and here are features of the situation which give us confidence. I would not like to appear to you as a prophet of evil or of sad things. I never believed that we would build Palestine with Jeremiahs.

We have some comforting hope in the attitude of the United States, the attitude of British public opinion (in spite of what I said about the temporary difficulties– and I am sure they will pass) and the attitude, last but not least, of the Soviet Union. We were happy to read President Truman's message to Ibn Saud which, in very clear terms, gave expression to the attitude of the American Government to the development of the Jewish National Home. I was equally pleased to read and grateful for the statement of Mr. Gromyko in his thoughtful speech which could have been, I do not want to impart anything to him which is not so, but it could have been made by a Zionist. I am sure he is not a Zionist. I do not want to offend him that way, but the speech, nevertheless, was a good Zionist statement.

There is another feature of the situation which no doubt has drawn your attention. So far, the ability, finance, and all that you have seen erected here which constitutes the National Home, has been created with our own hands. That is something to which I would like to call the specific attention of this Committee. One of the greatest reproaches which is usually levelled at the Jew is "Oh, yes, he may be a very good fellow and all that and no doubt when you come into a country you are law-abiding, you pay your taxes, you do not steal, and so on. But you see there is something about you which we do not altogether relish. You always come when things are ready. You come into the second floor of the building. The foundation, the dirty work which you need in digging and laying the foundation, putting up the bricks and stones, and all that has been done by others. When it is all ready, and the rooms are nicely painted, and the pyjamas are on the bed, you step in and you hire an elegant suite, and here you are. We do not like it."

This is the reason why Jews are usually branded as parasites: parasites not in the ordinary sense of the word, but in this particular sense.

Well, here in Palestine there were marshes and we have drained them; there were stones and we have planted over them; there were no houses and we have built them; it was ridden with disease and we have cleared it. All that has been done here, from the modest cottage of the settler to the University on Mt. Scopus, is the work of Jewish planning, Jewish genius and of Jewish hands and muscles, not only of money and initiative. This gives us a certain amount of pride and confidence. Given a dog's chance, we could do as well as anybody else. I do not think we are better than anybody else; I do not think we are worse than anybody else. I think we are just as good and just as bad as the others. But the chances are different. And here was a chance, a remedial chance, a chance of political circumstance. I believe, and I want to underscore this, we have made, under the circumstances, the best of that chance.

There is something else to be said, and I am saying it in all humility. Other peoples have colonized great countries, rich countries. They found when they entered there backward populations. And they did for the backward populations what they did. I am not a historian, and I am not sitting in judgment on the colonizing activity of the various great nations which have colonized backward regions. But I would like to say that, as compared with the result of the colonizing activities of other peoples, our impact on the Arabs has not produced very much worse results than what has been produced by others in other countries. ...

I have warned the various Commissions before whom I have had the honour to speak. I hope I will not have to do it again — not that I do not appreciate sufficiently this honour, but I hope it will not be necessary. I told them in 1936: there are in this part of the world — meaning Central Europe, Germany, and other countries — people who are pent up without being able to move; the world for them is divided into two parts — the countries where they cannot live — and the countries they cannot enter — and they are doomed. This sombre prophecy of 1936 came true in 1942. ...

It is, therefore, for us no more a question of refugees alone. It is very important to save refugees. It is very important, as I pointed out, to save every Jewish soul we can, particularly now, when every Jew alive is a precious possession to us. But there are higher things at stake, and that is the survival of the Jews as a people, and this can be achieved only through independence in a Jewish State in this country — in part of this country. ...

It may appear to you somewhat daring, if I make a tentative proposal, but my experience and my contribution to the building of Palestine emboldens me to speak on the subject. There is no question about it that when Palestine was promised, when the Declaration was given, when the Mandate was written — and I should like to say that the Mandate was written not only when Mr. Balfour was Foreign Secretary, it was completed in its present form under Lord Curzon, and I am quoting Lord Curzon because Mr. Balfour might be considered as biased in favour of the policy in which he is the main author. By no stretch of the imagination could Lord Curzon be accused of any bias in that direction. Still, at that time by "Palestine" was understood "Palestine and Trans-Jordan". Then Trans-Jordan was cut-off. As you know, the size of Trans-Jordan is much greater than that of Palestine – more than three times. It was cut off, so to speak, at a moment's notice. And here is a sort of irony. First you amputate Palestine. You cut off a country which is three or four or five times the size of Palestine, and then you turn round on poor Zionists and tell them, you are a small country; you cannot bring any population there; you must displace others, and we cannot allow that, and so on. I do not think it is cricket. I do not think it is fair play. Either you do not cut it off, or if you have done it you cannot throw it in our face that we are trying to bring a population into a small country. In fact, what we have been trying to do since that time is, by ingenuity and scientific development, to increase the size of the country, and as you cannot increase it materially, or geographically, we have tried to increase it in such a way that we are trying to make two blades of grass grow where one blade has grown before; in fact, to make four tomatoes grow where one has been growing before by intensifying – sometimes over-intensifying and utilising every little knot and every nook and cranny in Palestine and making it produce human sustenance. That has been our business since Palestine has been amputated. But it has been done, and I am not harking back to it, and I even realise that today in order to have peace in this country, stability in the Middle East – and the Middle East is important not only for Jews and Arabs, but also for the whole of the civilised world – we have great responsibility not to disturb the peace in this part of the world.

Knowing all that, we are – I think I am speaking the mind of a great many Jews, after a great deal of hardship, after a great deal of testing, after a great deal of evaluating the possibility of what we can do, for a form of partition which would satisfy the just demands of both the Jews and the Arabs. We realise that we cannot have the whole of Palestine. God made a promise; Palestine to the Jews. It is up to the Almighty to keep His promise in His own time. Our business is to do what we can in a very imperfect human way. I do not like to play on the sentiment of the distinguished Indian representative who sits here. I should say partition, is à la mode. It is not only in small Palestine; it is in big India. But at least there you have something to partition. Here we have to do it with a microscope. There you can do it with a big knife.

What are the advantages of partition? It has, in my opinion, two great advantages. It is final and it helps to dispel some of the fears of our Arab friends. I am not saying that you would dispel easily all fears. Fear is not a matter of logic. It is a matter of emotion, and emotional reaction cannot be dispelled by logical performance. But at any rate we can do all we can in order to help in future to mitigate their fear. If it is final the Arabs will know and the Jews will know that they cannot encroach upon each other's domain. To us it means something else.

It means equality of status with our Arab neighbours: the most important requisite for good relations between us and them. As long as they consider us inferior in political status they will not be anxious to make peace with us. Therefore, it is a desirable solution, although it represents, as I have already pointed out, a new and great sacrifice on the part of the Jewish people. It cannot be whittled down, it cannot be bargained down, and the part of Palestine which would remain after partition must be something in which Jews could live and into which we could bring a million and a half people in a comparatively short time. It must not be a place for graves only, or graveyards, or, as you sometimes see on very full trains, "standing room only". Therefore I have a plea to make to this distinguished Committee. I respectfully pray that you will one to a decision of this kind, and above all see that this decision is carried out – and, carried out quickly.

SPECIAL COMMITTEE ON PALESTINE
VERBATIM RECORD OF THE TWENTY-FIRST MEETING (PUBLIC)
Held at the Y.M.C.A. Building
Jerusalem, Palestine
Tuesday, 8 July 1947

IV

Sir Abdur RAHMAN (India): Rabbi Fishman, I do not know the Bible, I do not pretend to know it, but I should like to get information from you, your point of view, and I hope you will enlighten me as to what you have to say in regard to a few matters which I will put to you. Rabbi Fishman, what was "the Promised Land"?

Rabbi FISHMAN [Jewish Agency]: The Promised Land was quite a large one, from the river of Egypt up to the Euphrates.

Sir Abdur RAHMAN (India): It included the whole of Syria.

Rabbi FISHMAN: Yes, a part.

Sir Abdur RAHMAN (India): The whole of Trans-Jordan and Iraq?

Rabbi FISHMAN: No.

Sir Abdur RAHMAN (India): The whole of Syria, Lebanon, present Palestine and Trans-Jordan?

Rabbi FISHMAN: Yes, possibly part of Syria and Lebanon.

Sir Abdur RAHMAN (India): When was the promise made by God?

Rabbi FISHMAN: The promise was given to Abraham, Isaac and Jacob, about 4000 years ago.

Sir Abdur RAHMAN (India): When was it confirmed by God?

Rabbi FISHMAN: It was reaffirmed to Moses.

Sir Abdur RAHMAN (India): Did God also promise that twelve tribes would arise out of Ishmael, son of Hagar and Abraham?

Rabbi FISHMAN: It was definitely stated, the sons of Isaac would inherit the land.

Sir Abdur RAHMAN (India): That was not the question. Did God promise that twelve tribes would arise out of Ishmael or not?

Rabbi FISHMAN: He said not. Twelve tribes would arise only out of Jacob the son of Isaac.

Sir Abdur RAHMAN (India): When did Cyrus, the Persian king, order the Jews to return to Jerusalem?

Rabbi FISHMAN: It was approximately 2400 years ago.

Sir Abdur RAHMAN (India): Was not the promise of God made to Abraham and Moses fulfilled by Cyrus' order of return to Jerusalem?

Rabbi FISHMAN: Cyrus gave only a part of the land to the Jews.

Sir ABDUR RAHMAN (India): And therefore, according to you, a part of the promise of God was redeemed.

Rabbi FISHMAN: Maccabeans enlarged the area that Cyrus gave back to the Jews. Cyrus put in his proposal to Jews only a part of the country and the Maccabeans later expanded that part.

Sir ABDUR RAHMAN (India): Did the Arab Prince Yoshan object to the Jews return with Cyrus' order and try to stop them?

Rabbi FISHMAN: After the exile, many of the neighbouring peoples occupying a part of Palestine resisted the return of the Jews. Among them was also the gentleman mentioned by the representative of India.

Sir ABDUR RAHMAN (India): According to the Jews, was their return to this country not to take place with the appearance of the Messiah?

Rabbi FISHMAN: No, in accordance with the Jewish tradition the Jews should return to Palestine before the Messiah comes, and Jerusalem should be a part of Palestine. Only then, after the return of the Jews to Palestine in accordance with the tradition, the Messiah may arrive.

Sir ABDUR RAHMAN (India): How long after the return of the Jews will the Messiah arrive, according to you?

Rabbi FISHMAN: That is a thing nobody can tell.

Sir ABDUR RAHMAN (India): How long has Rabbi Fishman been in Palestine?

Rabbi FISHMAN: Forty-one years.

Sir ABDUR RAHMAN (India): How many synagogues were there in Palestine up to 1917?

Rabbi FISHMAN: I cannot give the exact figure for the moment, but in Jerusalem there were about fourteen synagogues.

Sir ABDUR RAHMAN (India): And outside Jerusalem?

Rabbi FISHMAN: There were a lot in other places such as Jaffa, Hebron. Some not existing now, at Safad, Haifa, Tiberias and in all the Jewish villages.

Sir ABDUR RAHMAN (India): Are there any Christian "Jews" in the country?

Rabbi FISHMAN: It is not for me to answer. There may be Jews who are converted, but I do not mix with them.

Sir ABDUR RAHMAN (India): But are there any?

Rabbi FISHMAN: I do not know, because I do not mix with them.

Sir ABDUR RAHMAN (India): I am asking you if you recognize Christian Jews to be Jews. The Government does not treat them as Jews.

Rabbi FISHMAN: I think that a Jew, even if he has been converted and has committed to sin, is nevertheless a Jew and cannot free himself from the bondages of Judaism.

Sir ABDUR RAHMAN (India): So according to you, a Christian Jew is a Jew?

Rabbi FISHMAN: I wrote a long article about that. Jews who have committed a sin and have been converted cannot free themselves from the bondages of Judaism.

Sir ABDUR RAHMAN (India): So, according to you, all the Christians and all the Moslems are Jews?

CHAIRMAN: Are there any more questions?

Rabbi FISHMAN: That is your opinion, not mine.

Sir ABDUR RAHMAN (India): I am asking your opinion.

CHAIRMAN: We will content ourselves with this answer.

…

Mr. BEN-ZEVIE (Vaad Leumi): … Our right to Palestine is based upon our national history. Like any other nation we claim the elementary right to independence and we identify ourselves with the Jewish Agency demanding the establishment of a Jewish State in Palestine. Although in the course of our history we lost independence, we never gave up our entity as a nation, we never ceased hoping for our return to the Land and the restoration of our State. Only once in its history has this land had its independent statehood, and that was the Kingdom of Israel. The inhabitants who lived in the Land before the children of Israel came here never succeeded in laying the foundation to one political and cultural unit in Palestine. The Holy Scriptures and the living historical tradition of our nation tell us of the Jewish State established not only on the basis of common origin and background, but also of religion, culture, language and ideals. The Jewish State of Palestine existed for almost eleven centuries with small interruptions, from the days of Saul and David up to the darkest days of the destruction of the Temple by the Romans in the year 70 C.E. In spite of the fall of the independent state, the bulk of the Jewish population in Palestine survived for almost another six centuries and shattered remainders clinged to their land and persisted in carrying on the tradition of their people. None of the conquerors in the history of the country, be they Romans, Arabs, Mongols, Mamelukes, or Turks, cared or succeeded in establishing a State, with the exception of the Latin Kingdom which only for ninety years formed a unity of the Land.

We firmly believe that the restoration of independence of the Land of Israel is the historical destiny of the entire Jewish people. In our paper called "Three Historical Memoranda" we prove that the Jewish nation never interrupted its connection with Palestine. In a special chapter, dealing with the continuity of Jewish settlement in Palestine, we prove that there was a Jewish population in existence in Palestine throughout the generations who never departed from the Holy Land and its soil. Moreover, waves of immigration kept coming from the Western as well as the Eastern and Oriental Diaspora.

It is an historical fact that for centuries during the Arab rule, the Crusaders' and the Turkish period, the country remained a waste and disease-stricken land and a population amounting previously to 3,200,000 in the beginning of the seventh century dwindled down to 673,000 on the eve of the British occupation. Since then the population increased threefold, the whole population increased threefold; the Yishuv, that is the Jewish population, rose from some 60,000 to 640,000. A similar figure of increase was reached by the Arab sector, due both to natural increase and to immigration from neighbouring Arab countries. This was increased by nearly 600,000 during this time. It is remarkable that no similar increase and development took place in the neighbouring Trans-Jordan, originally under the same British Mandate, where general conditions are not very much different from western Palestine and where natural resources are even more plentiful than here.

What is Palestine for us and what is it for the Arabs? For us, it is the sole refuge, the harbour of salvation and the sole hope for our dispersed nation, whilst for the Arabs it is a negligible part of the vast Arab territories. Compared with the Arab territories in Asia alone it represents 0.8 per cent, if we include Arab countries in Africa, Palestine is only 0.4 per cent. Even Arab countries with such natural resources as [Iraq] have a density of 8 per square kilometre, Syria 15 per square kilometre. The vast Arab territories and their natural resources leave space for an enormous increase of the Arab population, and for their development they do not rely on this small country of 27,000 square kilometres, while the Asiatic Arab countries alone consist of 3,226,000 square kilometres with a total population of only about 14,900,000.

During the period of the Mandate the Jews made their supreme efforts to build up the country, believing that the process of reconstruction would be favoured and encouraged by the Mandatory according to the letter and the spirit of the Mandate. Instead, the policy of the White Paper of 1939 aimed at stopping further development, immigration and colonisation of the country. We are convinced that if we had had the liberty of taking charge of our own affairs, hundreds of thousands might have been brought to Palestine and been saved. Now we face the fact that over one million of those who survived the Nazi inferno are condemned to utter despair if they are not granted immediate facilities of immigration. The strong links between them and us, among them there are many of their own families, and the wish to be reunited increase their anguish. The homes of the Yishuv are kept open, in every settlement, in every village, in every town dwelling to receive saved brethren.

At the same time the position of Jewish minorities in the neighbouring countries is rapidly deteriorating, politically, culturally and economically. The development during the past twenty-five years of the newly established Arab States does not provide any chance for non-Arab minorities, be they Assyrians, Kurds or Jews. The sole hope of the Jewish minorities is the exodus. Our appeal to you is: Open the gates of our country.

Permit me, Mr. Chairman, to conclude with a citation of a prophet who prophesied three thousand years ago, Isaiah: (62.10 ff.) "Go through, go through the gates; prepare ye the way of the people; cast up, cast up the highway; gather out the stones; lift up a standard for the people. Behold, the LORD hath proclaimed unto the end of the world, 'Say ye to the daughter of Zion, Behold, the salvation cometh.'"

SPECIAL COMMITTEE ON PALESTINE
VERBATIM RECORD OF THE TWENTY-FOURTH MEETING (PUBLIC)
Held at the Y.M.C.A. Building
Jerusalem, Palestine
Wednesday, 9 July 1947

V

Mr. MAGNES (Ihud Association): ... We propose that Palestine become a bi-national country composed of two equal nationalities, the Jews and the Arabs, a country where each nationality is to have equal political powers, regardless of who is the majority or the minority. We call this "Political: Parity".

Majority rule is, to be sure, the accepted working rule in countries which are uni-national as, for example, in the United States, but majority rule is not the universal working rule in multi-national countries such as Belgium, Canada, Czechoslovakia, Soviet Russia, Switzerland, Yugoslavia, where the equality of basic national rights of the different nationalities making up the state is protected against majority rule. It will not do, therefore, to try to apply to a country like Palestine the working rule of the majority in some such way as is done in countries of the West. Bi-nationalism based on parity is a comparatively new way. It gives full protection to the various religions of the country, to the national languages, cultures, institutions, and yet, with all of that, there is full allegiance to the political state. Switzerland proves this possible. That, to be sure, is not so new, it is over one hundred years old. In Switzerland, there are three or four basic nationalities. There is no concurrence of religion, language, nationality in the twenty-two cantons. Some of them are divided up. Nevertheless, we find in Switzerland this great experiment that has been succeeding for more than one hundred years, of three distinct nationalities, each one guarding their own culture jealously, and at the same time, proving faithful citizens of the political state.

We contend that multi-nationalism is a high ideal. It is not just something that is made to order to cover a given situation. The old way of having a major people and a minor people in a state of various nationalities we regard as reactionary. It will not do to have a dominant people and a dominated people. That leads to constant friction, breaks out in revolution, results in war. Parity, we contend, is the one just relationship between the different nationalities of a multi-national state.

It is not always easy to achieve a bi-national or multi-national state. In Palestine great concessions have to be made by all concerned. What are the concessions that the Arabs would have to make? They would have to yield their ambition to set up in Palestine a uni-national independent sovereign state. There are other Arab states which are uni-national, independent, sovereign. Yet in yielding that great ambition of theirs, which is only natural and to be understood, they would enjoy the maximum of national freedom in a bi-national Palestine equally with their Jewish fellow-citizens.

What are the concessions that the Jews would have to make? They would have to give up their dream of a uni-national independent sovereign Jewish state. That is a great concession. This is the only country where such a thing is conceivable. Yet a bi-national Palestine based upon parity between the two nationalities would give the Jews what they have not in any other place. It would make them a constituent nation in this country. They would not be classified as a minority, because in the bi-national state, based upon parity, there is no such thing politically as majority.

We have seen how the minority guarantees of the Treaty of Versailles broke down at every point.

Minorities can be protected only through parity, and the Jewish case, the Jewish cause in Palestine, can be protected here upon the basis of bi-nationalism with two equal nationalities, so that they are in Palestine not a minority – to be sure, not a majority, and they, too, can have full national rights equally with their Arab fellow citizens.

...

[T]he question of Jewish immigration is in many ways the crux of the whole situation. We propose three principles upon which Jewish immigration is to be encouraged. You will note that I say "encouraged".

First, that Jewish immigration be permitted up to parity with the Arabs. We call this numerical parity. What I have been describing before is, I said, what we call political parity. This would enable the Jews to bring in another 500,000 to 600,000 immigrants. The second principle would be that Jewish immigration be regulated in accordance with the economic absorptive capacity of the country. Third, that this economic absorptive capacity of the country be enlarged through a Development Plan, which is to be of benefit to all the inhabitants of the country.

...

CHAIRMAN [Emil Sandström, Sweden]: ... I shall only mention one difficulty, which I think might be the greatest, and that is this. When you state that the Arab standpoint, the Arab ambition, as you put it, is self-government, that is true; but I wonder whether the Arabs, in self-government, do not also put in a notion of proprietorship to the country and that they feel the Jewish immigration here is an invasion, a penetration, and that they resent this immigration. My question is whether the Arabs, in the scheme you propose, resent the insertion of this immigration as a condition of the cooperation. It is just the opposite of their aim, I think.

Mr. MAGNES: You are right in saying that that is the chief objection the Arabs have to the Jews – that the Jews are coming here in too large numbers. And from a certain point of view, when they use the term "invasion" it may be right. People are coming from the outside who were not born here, and that might perhaps conceivably be called an invasion. We have great sympathy with the Arab fear of Jewish domination. That is what it arrives at. We do not believe that the Arabs ought to be dominated by the Jews. We do not think Palestine is a place for that. But we do not think that the Jews ought to be dominated by the Arabs. If we come here as invaders – to use that very harsh term – it is not because we have found a new continent, as the early American settlers who found great riches before them and who wiped out the Indians in order to make a place for themselves in those vast spaces. We have not come into this country for wealth, because it can hardly be called a wealthy country from the material point of view. The wealth that is here we have more or less created by taking advantage of some of the natural resources which heretofore had been supposed not to exist as, for example, water. We have not come here because we happened to find on the map a country in 1917 where there were 800,000 inhabitants and which perhaps might hold 4,000,000; where the inhabitants are weak and we are going to overcome and dispossess them.

Why is it that we do it? Why is it that there are some of these younger men and women among the Jews who have no need whatsoever, materially or even spiritually, of migrating from their homes? It is because this is Palestine. It is because this is Eretz Israel. It is because we have these links with this country. If the Arabs want to deny the substantiality of these spiritual links, that is of course their affair, but we think that these spiritual links are just as substantial as the Kushan [Ottoman land deed] which my former landlord had, in the house where I lived, throughout his family for almost six hundred years. Before Columbus went to America his family had that title deed to that land. That is a mighty strong claim that he has. We contend that our claim is at least as strong – to be sure, not so material. This happens to be an instance where the Jewish people, which is accused of being a materialist people, is trying to emphasize spiritual bonds and trying to make these spiritual historic bonds of equal validity at least with these material Kushans or deeds, which certain landlords have over the soil.

You have put the problem from the Arab point of view, and you must consider it from that point of view. I have tried to give you an answer from our point of view. There are some who criticize us and say that the Arab natural rights, as we have called them, are not to be considered as of equal validity with Jewish historical rights. Our whole conception is to try to make this something that is equal–equality. There may be a certain amount of artificiality in that. If you weigh the thing, if it were capable of being weighed – these natural rights and these historical rights – heaven knows to which side the scale would tip. But this is a human situation and we think that situation can be met more or less successfully if we say to both of these peoples, both of whom have very good claims to this country: your claims are just; your claims have equal validity; now let us try to see if we cannot build up a common life together from that common background.

CHAIRMAN: You spoke of the somewhat artificial character of this principle of equality. That makes me ask another question. Would not the Arabs resent this artificial character of some of the most important principles of the constitution? Would they not say that they had been conceived with the aim of keeping them down? I mean, I suppose they have the majority now in the country, and they could say that these principles aim at depriving them of this majority situation.

Mr. MAGNES: These principles do deprive the Arabs of what a majority has in uni-national states. If Palestine were an Arab state and the Arabs were in the majority, they would be the rulers of the state; they would be the dominant people, the Jews the dominated people. If this were a Jewish state and the tables were reversed, the Jews would be the dominant people and the Arabs the dominated people. We have tried to avoid that. We have tried to set up the principle of multi-nationalism. It is not a principle which we ourselves have invented. There is a great literature to be studied on that principle. We quoted at least three books in some of our documents, all of them published in 1945: one on "Nationalism and Nationalities", by Professor Janovsky of New York; another "Eastern Europe between the Wars, 1918-1941" by Professor H. Seton-Watson; and another by Mr. A. Cobban on "National Self-Determination". It is not as though the situation in Yugoslavia, for example, which is the newest of the multi-national countries, were the same as in Switzerland, or that the situation in the Soviet Union were the same as in Belgium. The situation in Palestine is different from what it is in any of these, but there is this basic guiding principle of which we are advocates. We contend that this principle is a lofty principle. It is lofty because it tries to do away with domination by a majority over a minority. And it is lofty because it tries to find a practical way of bringing together different types of human beings. It is history that has created that. It is history that has created this congeries of nationalities in the Balkans, for example, and in this country and in other countries. No one of us has created that. The question is, how are we going to try to meet that historical situation?

We contend that you have to have a principle. That principle is the principle of bi-nationalism. Within that principle you will have to find very many ingenious methods of meeting certain practical, day-to-day difficulties. We have tried to outline some of those – by no means all of them – and it is for that reason that we suggest that there be a Commission on constitution, which is to work through and take its time in working through the details of this bi-national or multi-national state.

CHAIRMAN: I look at the question the whole time from the point of view of the practical workability, and from that point of view I ask this question also. Would not this artificial character of the principle of equality of which we have spoken give from the outset an invidious character to the constitution on the Arab side?

Mr. MAGNES: It might well be. There are Arabs who say that. On the other hand, there are Arabs – and I can testify to this from my personal experience – who are altogether in favour of this bi-national idea of two equal peoples in Palestine. If there is another answer that is better than this, then that other answer ought to be applied. We think there is no better answer and we think therefore that the best must be made of this principle of bi-nationalism or of multi-nationalism.

CHAIRMAN: Would it not have been a good thing for the success of your idea – of your scheme – if it had been put to trial at an earlier stage – let us say ten years ago?

Mr. MAGNES: You would not think that I was trying to be amusing if I said it would have been better if it had been tried twenty-five years ago.

CHAIRMAN: What I am aiming at is whether the situation has not deteriorated.

Mr. MAGNES: It has deteriorated almost from year to year.

CHAIRMAN: And also, we may say, from the time when the Anglo-American Committee made its inquiry.

Mr. MAGNES: It has deteriorated in certain respects since then, I think, primarily because of the failure to grant the 100,000 immigration certificates. On the other hand, since the Anglo-American Committee has been here there have been discussions of the problem on the Arab side, not altogether in the spirit of the present Arab Higher Committee. I think you will find from some of the discussions of the Arab League, or from some of the members of the Arab League, a much more moderate attitude towards these proposals of ours than the present intransigent position of the Arab Higher Committee. But you are right; the situation has deteriorated. The situation has deteriorated technically in my view since the Jewish Agency adopted as its official programme the Jewish State for Palestine.

...

CHAIRMAN: ... Is it not right to say that the anxiety of the Arabs has been aroused by this claim for a Jewish State?

Mr. MAGNES: There is no question of it.

CHAIRMAN: That the exasperation on both sides, has increased?

Mr. MAGNES: Yes.

CHAIRMAN: That there is a rather nervous state of affairs here?

Mr. MAGNES: Yes.

CHAIRMAN: But you do not think it is too late to put your idea to a test?

Mr. MAGNES: It is never too late to do a good thing.
...

Mr. MAGNES: We do not look upon Palestine as a place where once and for all you can put a stamp of finality. Moreover, if you have in a Jewish partitioned state a tremendous – and you can have no Jewish partitioned state without a tremendous Arab minority, an Arab minority almost as large as the Jewish majority itself – you would there have the same bi-national problem. Why not then, in all of Palestine. Why use the term "finality" in all of this? Why try to say that a problem as complex as this, an historical problem that has been developing for hundreds, perhaps, one might say for thousands of years, is to be met by some formula that will overnight, from today to tomorrow pronounce: "The problem is settled now once and for all"? We do not contend that our solution is a settlement of this problem once and for all. We merely contend that it gives the framework for the development of common interests between the Jews and the Arabs, who are both going to remain here unless the Arabs drive the Jews into the sea, as they say they once drove the Crusaders into the sea, or the Jews drive the Arabs into the desert, as some think perhaps they should be driven.

...

Mr. RAND (Canada): What would you say about the development of what is called the concept of nationality among both groups? I ask that because essentially it is the impingement upon that sensibility in all governmental arrangements that produces, I would think, most of the antagonisms.

Mr. MAGNES: If you knew a way of wiping that problem out –

Mr. RAND (Canada): I was wondering how sensitive it is in this country.

Mr. MAGNES: It is very sensitive. Both the Jews and the Arabs are novices in relation to the feelings of nationality. The Jews always have held together by an invisible national bond, but by a more visible religious bond, so that when one talks of the bond of nationality among the Jews, one talks of a comparatively modern phenomenon. It is even more modern among the Arabs. The Arab awakening from the point of view of nationality, is a comparatively recent development.

Mr. RAND (Canada): Would you think it became more or less sensitive as it developed and became more mature?

Mr. MAGNES: That has been the case I think, with every developing sense.

Mr. RAND (Canada): Would you say that was so in Central Europe?

Mr. MAGNES: I would say it was so in Central Europe, so much so that – but what do you mean by Central Europe?

Mr. RAND (Canada): I have in mind the old Austro-Hungarian Empire.

Mr. MAGNES: They have had their fill. For them, national sensibility was no new thing. It was something that had grown stale in their mouths, something that had brought them nothing but pain and suffering, and for that reason the sensibility as to nationality in Austria-Hungary, for example, was, so I believe, a declining thing. This sensibility as to nationality among the Jews and among the Arabs is still on the rise. There are Jews who have passed beyond that sensibility. More of them I think, many more of them, than among the Arabs, because the Jews have had the experience of the disadvantages of this national sensibility; they have experienced it in their own lives, trying to work through their own problems of Jewish nationality, and they have come to the conclusion that that is not perhaps the final answer to things anyway. Nationality is something that undoubtedly still requires a great deal of clarification, but to answer your question as to this situation here: there is undoubtedly that sensibility as to a feeling of nationality which makes the problem here much more difficult.

...

Sir Abdur RAHMAN (India): Dr. Magnes, can you suggest any other solution for parity than what you have suggested? Can it not be secured, for instance, by constitutional safeguarding of the rights of the various parties without affecting the numerical parity between the two sections of the community living there?

Mr. MAGNES: Does your question mean to imply that there would be no further Jewish immigration?

Sir Abdur RAHMAN (India): No, it does not imply that.

Mr. MAGNES: Then I do not understand the question.

Sir Abdur RAHMAN (India): Taking the situation as a whole today, the question whether there is going to be future immigration or not may be left to be determined by the state which will come onto being later on. But to settle the question today, is it not possible to achieve the same objective by safeguarding the civil, political and religious rights and liberties by constitution, and by providing that no change in the constitution should be effected unless something like seven-eighths or four-fifths of the majority vote for the change?

Mr. MAGNES: What you say has a great deal to it. On the other hand, I would like to ask you when that would begin? What would happen to Jewish immigration meanwhile? If I understand you alright, you would leave the determination of the problem of immigration to that bi-national state based on parity when it came into being. Now, I ask when will it come into being? What will happen to the Jews in these intervening years? If that state could come into being at once, then I would say that what you have proposed has a great deal to it. But there is no guarantee that that will happen.

Sir ABDUR RAHMAN (India): But suppose it is that independence be granted to Palestine and the Mandatory Power and the Trusteeship disappear altogether. I am just putting the idea before you to consider whether or not it is practical – we will go into details later on. Supposing independence is recognized for Palestine as such and a bi-national state is brought into being, and that that state is given the safeguards against political, religious and other liberties, will power be given to that constitution which comes into being in pursuance of that recommendation, if it is adopted by the Assembly, to settle the question itself?

Mr. MAGNES: Is that a bi-national state based on parity?

Sir ABDUR RAHMAN (India): That is what I am saying.

Mr. MAGNES: Is it based on parity?

Sir ABDUR RAHMAN (India): That is what I am asking you. That is the very question. Can we, without resorting to numerical parity, safeguard against the minority who are numerically less?

Mr. MAGNES: I don't think so. I think the history of the past generation has taught us that the safeguarding of minority rights is just nothing but words. The safeguarding of minority rights in the various countries where Jews were minorities, and where their rights were to be safeguarded, failed. That is the basis of our contention. We contend that there is one just, equitable, practicable way of meeting a minority-majority problem, and that is by wiping it out and making both the majority and the minority equal constituent partners.

Sir ABDUR RAHMAN (India): Although numerically they may not be so?

Mr. MAGNES: Although numerically they may not be so. A numerical majority, we contend, is all right for this place and for that place, but it has not been decreed from Heaven for other places. And if one starts on the assumption that a numerical majority is going to be bound by a constitutional provision to protect the minority, history teaches us that the majority sooner or later becomes arrogant, becomes dominant, and, subjects the minority to its will. It then has the civil service in its hands. It has the military in its power. It has diplomatic representation in its power. It has economic key positions in its power. It can wipe the minority out, if it wants to. And if there is any virtue in any constitution, it must be just that – that there be no minority and that there be no majority. There is, to be sure, the logical contradiction that was pointed out by the gentleman on the other side of the table but we have faced that logical contradiction and we think that our formula of parity is a formula that can be accepted by both the Jews and the Arabs. And, we know Arabs who do accept it.

...

Mr. SIMIC (Yugoslavia): Dr. Magnes, you said that the Jewish nationality presupposed birth in the Jewish nation, if I have properly understood you. Are you sure that during the centuries there have been no conversions and that all existing Jews have been born into the Jewish nation?

Mr. MAGNES: By no means. There have been many conversions to Judaism, and they are all Jews, and their children are Jews. Their children are, I should say, members of the Jewish nation. Whether they are or not, I am ready to include them also in the Jewish nation, although nationality to me conveys in some way or other also the conception of birth. But, there have been conversions by the tens of thousands.

...

Mr. MAGNES: If you are going to have a central administering body, then you have almost a federation. If you have a central administering body, you have the Jewish State here and the Arab State there. It does not matter much what you call them, province or state, or whatever else, and the central administering body is then to be the important thing.

Mr. RAND (Canada): Well, necessarily? I am dealing purely hypothetically now. Suppose the fundamental administrative departments were land and immigration. Suppose those were committed to the States.

Mr. MAGNES: You mean that each State could deal with its own immigration and each State could deal with its own land?

Mr. RAND (Canada): Yes.

Mr. MAGNES: What would then be the part of the central administering authority?

Mr. RAND (Canada): Well, those features that have been mentioned, the customs, foreign trade, inter-communications of all sorts, works that affect both States.

Mr. MAGNES: Well, that is practically what the Morrison-Grady Plan proposed. The Morrison-Grady Plan said that in the Jewish province we will be in control of immigration; we will be in control of land. In the Arab province, the Arabs will be in control of immigration and of land. It may be that you have in mind some modification of the Morrison-Grady Plan.

Mr. RAND (Canada): Well, I am suggesting a modification of the field of central power, a lessening of it, a minimum. What is the fundamental objection to that?

Mr. MAGNES: Well, the fundamental objection, to my mind, is that it segregates Arabs and Jews.

Mr. RAND (Canada): In a federal state, of course, the whole of the land is yours. I am a Canadian living in one of the provinces, but my Canadianism extends from the Atlantic to the Pacific.

Mr. MAGNES: There you have a strong central government, have you not?

Mr. RAND (Canada): In that instance, yes. But the interest, the spread of the individual's conception over the total commonwealth, you might call it, is not affected by the fact that you have two states in which the residue of power may be committed to the state rather than to the central government.

Mr. MAGNES: Well, if I understand your point, it is this: That you would set up a joint commonwealth, an Arab or Jewish commonwealth with a central –

Mr. RAND (Canada): I am suggesting that as a possibility.

Mr. MAGNES: I understand. I would like to try to understand it and to meet it. You are setting up a joint commonwealth, Arab-Jewish, and you are giving to the Arab state or province certain functions and powers and the same practically to the Jewish. That is one way of doing it. There is no question about that. That is the essence of the Morrison-Grady Plan, except that you would whittle down the central powers that are so obtrusive in the Morrison-Grady Plan, all of them remaining in the hands of the British there. You would make the central powers limited in extent and confine them probably to water and to other matters of common interest. The objection I have to that is this: You nevertheless set up boundaries. And, as I tried to indicate this morning, boundaries are not only difficult to draw up but they are dangerous to maintain. You set up boundaries on either side of which the Jewish youth and the Arab youth are going to be trained in chauvinism and you make the creation of irredentism on either side of these boundaries a very simple thing. …

Mr. RAND (Canada): Well, even you suggested boundaries of counties.

Mr. MAGNES: Yes, but those are purely local administrative boundaries.

Mr. RAND (Canada): What do you think these suggested boundaries would do in the way of impediments or obstacles to each group?

Mr. MAGNES: The local administrative boundaries?

Mr. RAND (Canada): Yes.

Mr. MAGNES: There would be absolutely no need of a passport from one county to another.

Mr. RAND (Canada): There would not be in the case I suggested. You would be citizens, in effect, of the commonwealth.

Mr. MAGNES: Well, that is an entirely different conception from what I understand partition to be.

Mr. RAND (Canada): I quite agree.

Mr. MAGNES: I see. So we have been arguing at cross purposes, really.

Mr. RAND (Canada): No.

Mr. MAGNES: If you want to set up a commonwealth, call it bi-national. Why not?

Mr. RAND (Canada): Well, I think it is a question of names, so far as that goes.

Mr. MAGNES: Yes, all right, do or do not call it bi-national. If you want to set up this commonwealth, give freedom of access to all citizens, to all parts of this commonwealth, and freedom for land purchase in all parts of that commonwealth.

Mr. RAND (Canada): You might have to qualify that. I was speaking of the right of any individual in the commonwealth to go where he pleased. Now that is a fundamental privilege. On the other hand, as each state would have control over its land and immigration, in fact, the geographical boundary would operate as the control of the numerical population.

Mr. MAGNES: That is one of the things I would object to, that each state should have control over its lands. I would like to see a condition under which I could have land anywhere in this country, and an Arab could have land anywhere in this country.

Mr. RAND (Canada): Of course, I agree that that might be desirable, but I am not losing sight of the fact that no matter what is suggested, there will be objections to it. I was wondering whether we could not make progress towards that which might be least objectionable.

Mr. MAGNES: You might find it less objectionable to the Arabs; but you will find it very objectionable, in the eyes of the Jews, to be excluded from lands here, there, and everywhere. ... That is one of the reasons why I would not want them to accept partition.

...

Mr. RAND (Canada): Loyalties must cluster around ideas, or feelings; at least sentiments. Here, it seems to me that we are lacking in the framework of a conception in which loyalty in a Palestinian sense can arise. I think it was the Peel Commission that said it was nonsense to think that either the Jews or the Arabs in the present condition of things took any pride in Palestine, or even contemplated his relation to it as that of a citizen of one state. Now could you modify that by a change in setting?

Mr. MAGNES: Might I read you the last paragraph in our statement to the Anglo-American Committee? It is headed "A Palestine Solution":

"What a boon to mankind it would be if the Jews and the Arabs of Palestine were to strive together to make their Holy Land into a thriving, peaceful Switzerland, situated at the heart of this ancient highway between East and West. A 'Palestine Solution' is required for the Palestine problem. This would have an incalculable political and spiritual influence in all the Middle East and far beyond. A bi-national Palestine could become a beacon of peace in the world."

What I may say is that one of our problems is the creation of just those loyalties that you so rightly emphasize. A loyalty for a Palestine State and not just for a Jewish State or for an Arab State. If that be our ideal, the question is how is it to be brought about, and it seems to me that the fewer barriers set up between the Arabs and the Jews – territorial or political or economic – the better chance you have of creating common loyalties for this Palestine State.

Mr. RAND (Canada): Yes, the only question would be whether the one or the other practically is realizable. Which would be the more likely to attract that new conception of loyalty which is a necessary condition, but which seems today to be absent?

Mr. MAGNES: … What is the higher ideal and what is the more likely ideal to be carried out? That is the question you ask. Now I would like to answer that. It may be that any answer that is given will have more or less to be imposed by the United Nations. The question is what can be imposed with least difficulty? That is the way I should like to formulate [it]. I think partition cannot be imposed. It is going to create war. The great majority of the Arabs are against it. Large numbers of Jews, both extremists and moderates, and among the religious groups of the Jews, are against it. It is going to create these irredenta and these outbursts. The bi-national state, however, is here. We are a bi-national state. We do not have to draw any new boundaries. We do not have to persuade anybody that that part of the country is land for the Arabs and this part of the country is land for the Jews. It would hardly have to be imposed. It will come into being. If you begin with the appointment, for example, of a Jew and an Arab – take the most modest of all requirements – as members of the Executive Council, sitting with the High Commissioner of this country during the period of the Mandate, that is nothing that you will have to go to war for, or all these other things that I tried to outline in the government of the country. Those things arise almost naturally. They are organic. You do not have to segregate people in any sense of the term, physically or spiritually, so that I have not the slightest doubt myself that if anything is to be imposed, the one thing that can be imposed is the bi-national state, because using the word imposed about that is a very strong term. We are here already a bi-national state, and any attempt to make these divisions is going to be something that will stir up animosity, that does not at the present time exist.

…

Mr. RAND (Canada): I was thinking of the more or less universal objective or dream or, you might say, spiritual aim of the Jewish people to have some part of this earth's surface which it might say was its own exclusively.

Mr. MAGNES: Well, if it were all left to me and we had a free hand, I would create a Jewish State. I am not among those who have objections in principle to a Jewish State. There are many Jews throughout the world in America and elsewhere who object to a Jewish State in principle. I am not one of those. I would like to see the Jewish people burdened with the task of conducting a state. They might, perhaps, add to the spiritual treasures of mankind if they were given that burden. But it has not been left to me. There is no tabula rasa. We are here in this country with two peonies. One of the ways of trying to evade that has been to try to find some other territory. The British Government at one time offered the Jews a settlement in Uganda. The Jewish people refused that settlement. Why? Because it was not Palestine. There may be other countries in the world which would offer space for Jewish homeless people. The Jewish people are not interested in that. I must say I am surprised some of the great countries of the world have not opened their gates to some of the

Jewish displaced persons, but all constantly concentrated only and exclusively on Palestine for the reception of these unhappy languishing victims of this terrible holocaust. But the Jewish people would turn it all down. When I say the Jewish people, I mean Jewish history, I mean the Jewish future, would turn it down as it has turned it down thus far. So that we find ourselves in this peculiar position, a peculiar people, that is what we are called in our Bible – and we are a peculiar people, sometimes in the good sense and sometimes, perhaps, not in so good a sense – and this is a peculiar land, with, as we have agreed, millions of people interested in it, and it is here we want to set up our National Home for good and true purposes and where we are setting up our National Home.

Now if you think that by this division, this partition, you are answering the century-long yearning of the Jewish people for a niche in the world, for a home, for their own state, I think myself that is a mistaken conception. This does not answer the Jewish need for that. It is too small. It has too large a minority of Arabs in that particular state, too many administrative, economic, social and educational difficulties. If you could give to the Jewish people Palestine, all of Palestine, as many of our Jews want – we have our parties who say that of this talk, all our talk and the partition talk and the rest of it is all rot; what the Jewish people require is Palestine on both sides of the Jordan River – and some go as far as the Euphrates River, because in our Bible the boundaries of Palestine have been set at times from the River of Egypt to the Euphrates River – (which you could not do, of course) – that, perhaps, might meet this great historical need of the Jewish people for some kind of a state that would make this the equivalent in statehood of some of the other peoples of the world. But to take this tiny country – you have seen how small it is.

Mr. RAND (Canada): It necessarily has to be symbolic, by its geographical limits, but what you say is that that yearning must remain forever unsatisfied.

Mr. MAGNES: I say this, that as long as Palestine is inhabited by two peoples and as long as we have not had one or two generations of experience and of experiment, of hit-and-miss, of working things out together – I say that the Jewish people will have to do without that as it has done without that for many hundreds of years. I am convinced in my own heart that the Jewish people here can be creative that is what we are after, most of all. In addition, by increasing immigration up to parity in this bi-national state, even though we do not achieve our legitimate ambition to have one state in the world that we may call our own, I am sure the solution will be more easily found. I do not think the task could be accomplished otherwise.

SPECIAL COMMITTEE ON PALESTINE
VERBATIM RECORD OF THE THIRTIETH MEETING (PUBLIC)
Held at the Y.M.C.A. Building
Jerusalem, Palestine
Monday, 14 July 1947

VI

Mr. FRANGIE (Minister for Foreign Affairs of the Lebanon) (translation from French): Mr. Chairman, Members of the Committee, the Governments of the Arab States, though convinced that there is only one solution for the Palestinian problem, namely, cessation of the Mandate and independence for Palestine, and that any investigation of so obvious a question has become unnecessary, nevertheless warmly welcomed the invitation of your Committee, as representative of the highest international authority the world has yet known. The Governments of the Arab States are persuaded that the Committee, desirous of establishing the conditions necessary for international cooperation, as the result of its investigation will adopt recommendations in conformity with the principles of self-determination and independence consecrated by the United Nations Charter.

The Governments of the Arab States do not intend to enumerate in this Memorandum all the arguments in support of the Palestine case. They will confine themselves to drawing the Committee's attention to two main points:

1. Palestine's right to self-determination.
2. The need to maintain peace in the Middle East.

I. <u>Palestine's right to self determination</u>
When the Balfour Declaration was issued, envisaging the establishment of a Jewish national home and opening the way for Zionist immigration, the Arabs formed 93% of the population of Palestine. The Declaration, which cannot in any case be considered valid as regards Arab Palestine, ignored Palestine's right

to self-determination both at the time it was issued and afterwards. Later, attempts were even made to silence the Arabs and bring them to an attitude of resignation. Far from stifling their claims, these attempts had the effect of strengthening their desire for liberation and their faith in the justice of their cause.

Their struggle for independence and for the safeguarding of their rights started at the beginning of this century with the natural awakening of the Arab peoples and the movement against Ottoman domination. They took part in this liberation movement and spared no effort or sacrifice. Together with the rest of the Arabs, they rose against the Turks, fighting alongside the Allies on all the battlefields of the Middle-East, in the Hedjaz, Palestine, Syria, the Lebanon, and Iraq.

As partners of the victorious Allies in 1918, they were entitled to enjoy the freedom for which the Allies had fought. But that freedom to which they aspired and for which they had fought was denied them; for reasons irrelevant to their case. Abruptly confronted by Zionist ambitions and Allied promises to satisfy them, the Arabs of Palestine were forced to turn their struggle against the Ottoman Empire into one against their own Allies.

The Allies renounced the promises they had made to the Arabs at the beginning of their struggle for independence, imposing a mandate system which is nothing less than colonization. And the strictest of the mandates was the one applied to Palestine.

In spite of the promises made in the course of hostilities, the mandate system imposed upon all the Arab countries which had formed part of the old Ottoman Empire was applied at the same time, in all its severity, to Palestine. Whereas by the texts of the Mandates for the Lebanon, Syria and Iraq, the Mandatory Power was under obligation to assist the mandated State and lead it towards independence, the principle of which had been recognized by Article 22 of the League of Nations Covenant [*see* Appendix], the text of the Mandate for Palestine provided for the establishment of a Jewish national home and opened the door to immigration and the settlement of foreign Jews in Palestine.

The Mandate thereby distorted the normal development of Arab Palestine and deflected the natural course of its history. In the attempt to recover their lost freedom and independence, the Palestinian Arabs found themselves compelled not only to throw off the yoke of foreign control but also to struggle against the inroads of a foreign population whose ultimate aim was to relegate them to a secondary position in their own country.

Whilst the people of Iraq were casting off the heavy burden of the Mandate and Syria and the Lebanon were freeing themselves from foreign occupation and gaining full independence and sovereignty, the situation in Palestine became steadily worse. Wave upon wave of Zionist immigrants streamed into the Holy Land. National liberation became nothing more than a mirage.

The origin of Palestine's troubles is to be found in two documents, which are null and valueless, although it is upon them that Zionist claims are based: the Balfour Declaration and the Mandate.

In the first of these documents, the British Government undertook to facilitate the establishment of a Jewish National Home, thereby violating the principle of self-determination and the rules of international law. At the time when the undertaking was given, Great Britain had no legal relations with Palestine, which then formed part of the Ottoman Empire. Further, the Balfour Declaration violates the undertakings given by the British Government concerning the Arabs in the letters exchanged between Sharif Hussein and Sir Henry McMahon, recognizing Arab independence within boundaries which included Palestine. Finally, the Balfour Declaration contravened the 1918 Declaration which stated that the British Army was entering Palestine not as a conquering but as a liberating army.

As for the Mandate, it contains the same redhibitory defects as the Balfour Declaration. It also violates Article 22 of the League of Nations Covenant. Whereas the Covenant states that the purpose of the Mandate is to serve the interests of the mandated territory and requires the Mandatory to lead it towards independence, the text of the Palestine Mandate envisages placing Palestine under such political, administrative and economic conditions as will secure the establishment of a Jewish National Home. The same article of the League of Nations Covenant provides for consultation of the inhabitants of the mandated territories. The inhabitants of Palestine were not consulted.

However, the American King-Crane Commission, which was sent to Palestine in 1919, expressed its views on the Balfour declaration in the following terms:

"For 'a national home for the Jewish People' is not equivalent to making Palestine into a Jewish State; nor can the erection of such a Jewish State be accomplished without the gravest trespass upon the civil and religious rights of existing non-Jewish communities in Palestine...The fact came out repeatedly in the Commission's conferences with Jewish representatives, that the Zionists looked forward to a practically complete dispossession of the present non-Jewish inhabitants of Palestine by various forms of purchase...To subject a people so minded to unlimited Jewish immigration...would be a gross violation of the principles (for which the Allied Powers had fought the war).

"The Peace Conference should not shut its eyes to the fact that the anti-Zionist feeling in Palestine and Syria is intense and not lightly to be flouted. No British officer, consulted by the Commissioners, believed that the Zionist programme could be carried out except by force of arms. The officers generally thought that a force of not less than 50,000 soldiers would be required...

"That of itself is evidence of a strong sense of the injustice of the Zionist program on the part of the non-Jewish populations of Palestine and Syria. Decisions requiring armies to carry them out are sometimes necessary but they are surely not gratuitously to be taken in the interests of serious injustice. For the initial claim often submitted by Zionist representatives, that they have a 'right' to Palestine, based on an occupation of 2,000 years ago, can hardly be seriously considered...

"It is to be remembered that the non-Jewish population of Palestine – nearly nine-tenths of the whole – is emphatically against the entire Zionist programme. The tables show that there was no one thing upon which the population of Palestine was more agreed than upon this...It must be believed that the meaning...of the complete Jewish occupation of Palestine has not been fully sensed by those who urge the extreme Zionist programme. It would intensify...the anti-Jewish feeling both in Palestine and in all other parts of the world which look to Palestine as the Holy Land."

The Zionists, however, were not satisfied with the Balfour Declaration or the Mandate, in spite of the extent to which these documents violate the sacred rights of the Arabs. They took advantage of the ambiguity of the texts in order to extinguish the very life of Arab Palestine.

Great Britain recognized the abnormal situation created by the conflicting Allied promises to the Arabs and Jews. She also recognized that in fulfilling her obligations as a Mandatory Power she came into conflict with the rights of the Arabs in their own country on the one hand, and on the other with the promises given in the Balfour Declaration, the result being to make application of that Mandate impossible. That is why she has referred the Palestine question to the United Nations.

In his concluding statement, after the failure of the last Conference on Palestine, Mr. Bevin said:
"We shall explain to the United Nations that the Mandate has proved to be unworkable in practice and that the obligations undertaken to the two communities in Palestine have proved to be irreconcilable."

That is proof that both the Balfour declaration and the Mandate were irregular and could not provide the basis for an acceptable legal situation; and that therefore the Arabs are entitled to reject them and to regard an interpretation of either as contrary to the elementary principles of justice and implying a threat to the most cherished of rights, their right to existence.

To sum up, the right to self-determination to which the Arab people of Palestine are entitled and which they should be able to exercise, has been continually violated and is still violated today. It is none the less a natural, absolute, inalienable right, which neither force nor "fait accompli" can remove; and it consecrates the Arab claims and condemns Zionist ambitions.

The Governments of the Arab States looking towards the democratic principles on which the United Nations was founded as the best defence and surest guarantee of that right, demand the full application of those principles in Palestine. They are convinced that the Special Committee would not envisage a solution violating that right or the principles of the United Nations.

II. <u>Threats to peace in the Middle East</u>
The attitude of the Arab Governments and peoples to Zionism is based, secondly, upon their anxiety to maintain peace in the Middle East. Peace there is threatened by the expansionist aims and terrorist methods of Zionism.

1) At the outset the Zionist movement was content merely to look to Palestine for a refuge. Then it demanded a National Home. Having obtained that, it sought to extend its domain and create a kind of state within the Palestinian State, with its own institutions and finances, its own economy and its own army. Now the Zionists are planning to establish a Jewish State on Palestinian territory, a State which will take in the whole of Palestine. And even before achieving that, they are already seeking to spread further at the expense of the neighbouring Arab States.

As far back as the 1918 Peace Conference, the Zionist Organization issued a memorandum, dated 3 February 1919, officially claiming the whole of Transjordan and part of Syria and the Lebanon, up to Saida, Jisr el-Karaon, Wadi-el-Tein and the Harmoun. In the course of negotiations which took place that same year between France and Great Britain, in their capacity of Mandatory Powers over the countries formerly belonging to the Ottoman Empire, the Zionist Organization demanded the extension of the northern frontiers of Palestine as far as the Litani River and the plains of Hauran and Jaulan in Syria.

These plans for territorial expansion have subsequently been supported in public. Every responsible Zionist leader, every Zionist doctrinaire and publicist has continually proclaimed that the boundaries of Palestine as drawn in 1919 were the "Mandate boundaries" which Zionism refuses to recognize and aims to extend considerably in the future.

Not long ago, on the occasion of the Histraduth elections at Haifa, in 1944, Mr. Ben Gurion publicly declared that the Jews who propose to settle in Palestine, by force if necessary, will not hesitate to extend the boundaries of the country, since the Jewish State demanded by the Zionists is not their movement's final goal but only a preliminary step thereto.

When at the beginning of 1946 the British Government made known its intention to recognize the independence of Trans-Jordan within its present boundaries, Mr. Shertok told the press, on 23 January 1946, that the Jewish Agency would make every possible effort to prevent the execution of this plan and that although the Zionists had not previously opposed the Mandate over Trans-Jordan, nevertheless they could not approve the final secession of Trans-Jordan from Palestine.

This statement by one of the heads of the Jewish Agency was officially expressed in a note to the British Secretary of State for the Colonies protesting against the proclamation of the independence of Trans-Jordan and stressing the fact that Trans-Jordan, which formed part of the territory under British Mandate, could only be considered as the eastern part of Palestine.

The Zionists did not fail to reveal to your Committee their organization's real intentions as regards the boundaries of Palestine. These intentions were clearly evident from the statements made by Mr. Shertok and Rabbi Fishman, who recalled that God had promised the Jews a land stretching from the peninsula of Sinai to the Euphrates.

2) Zionism however does not content itself with mere propaganda in favour of the fulfilment of its expansionist projects at the expense of the Arab countries. Its plan involves recourse to terrorism, both in Palestine and in other countries. It is known that a secret army has been formed with a view to creating an atmosphere of tension and unrest by making attempts on the lives of representatives of the governing authority and by destroying public buildings. The assassination of Lord Moyne in Egypt, the attacks on the British Embassy at Rome, the incidents of the King David Hotel and the Officers' Club in Jerusalem, the St. John of Acre prison, the destruction of road and rail communications and the kidnapping and flogging of British officers, are all examples of the terrorist methods instituted by the Zionist organizations for the purpose of gaining possession by violence of a country which is not theirs.

This aggressive attitude, resulting from the Mandatory Power's weakness in dealing with them, will not fail to give rise in turn to the creation of similar organizations by the Arabs. The responsibility for the disturbances which might result there from throughout the Middle East will rest solely with the Zionist organizations, as having been the first to use these violent tactics.

It is the hope of the Governments of the Arab States, however, that the situation of the Jewish communities in their country will not be affected thereby.

3) No State could tolerate mass immigration such as that to which Palestine is subjected. Immigration restrictions are established in all countries to protect the best interests of the country and the rights of the inhabitants. Thus the Canadian Government has just announced that it will admit only 5,000 foreign refugees to its vast territories. The Australian Government has also made known the fact that it will not permit the refugees admitted to its territory to form colonies and that they are to be distributed throughout the country in order that they may become assimilated. Similar measures have been taken in Norway and various other countries.

Your honourable Committee will surely have realized that the situation in Palestine is very unstable and contains within it the seeds of possible conflicts which may spread throughout the Middle East.

The Governments of the Arab States cannot remain indifferent to this state of affairs. The safety of their own country is at stake and this gives them the right to oppose Zionism by every means at their disposal and even makes it their duty to do so.

Moreover, Palestine has for centuries been an Arab country and its preservation as such is a prerequisite for the harmonious development of the peoples of the Middle East and for their cooperation in the work of world peace, and progress.

For ethnic, cultural, political and economic reasons, Palestine is in fact an integral part of this Arab world, which is organized into sovereign States bound together by the political and economic pact of 22 March 1945. This organization of States, which subscribes to the Charter of the United Nations, fulfils its aspirations in encouraging regional organizations and agreements.

Any breach in this union, any scission between the States of which it is composed, threatens to destroy it and to cause unrest and confusion in this particularly vulnerable part of the world.

4) The Jewish State which the Zionists are endeavouring to establish in Palestine is not moreover a viable State either from the political or from the economic point of view.

The Arab States could not, in fact, tolerate the creation of a State composed of foreign elements from so many parts, each with its own mentality, its insatiable desires, for the fulfilment of which they deliberately use violent and destructive means such as those we have mentioned.

Against a State established by violence the Arab States will be obliged to use violence; that is a legitimate right of self-defence. Moreover, the foreign State on Arab territory will not in any case be able to count upon the establishment of economic or any other relations with the neighbouring Arab States. A State created under such conditions could not but be doomed to failure.

Concluding remarks

The Governments of the Arab States firmly hope that the Committee will bear these considerations in mind and endeavour to propose such a solution as may put an end to the present unrest and ensure the triumph of justice and the establishment of peace. They feel sure that this solution could only be inspired by the democratic principles on which the United Nations is founded.

The first of these principles establishes respect for the independence of the peoples and their right of self-determination. The Arab people of Palestine demand above all their recognized liberty and sovereign independence. The Arab States unanimously grant their unreserved support in the achievement of these claims. They have already submitted definite proposals in this sense and today wish to stress once more one of these proposals because they attach the greatest importance to it and because it constitutes a basic condition which will not admit of any compromise.

This proposal consists of the necessity of stopping immediately all Jewish immigration into Palestine, of maintaining the regulations now in force with regard to land transfer and of creating, without delay, an independent Arab Government based on democratic principles.

The Governments of the Arab States are of the opinion that any plan involving partitioning, far from solving the Palestine dispute would only aggravate it. Any Jewish State established in Palestine would inevitably become a centre of intrigue and a rallying-point for the Zionist forces, which are to be hurled against the Arab countries. The Governments of the Arab States will not under any circumstances agree to permit the establishment of Zionism as an autonomous state on Arab territory, towards which hundreds of thousands of foreign immigrants would stream.

They wish to state that they feel certain that the partition of Palestine and the creation of a Jewish State would result only in bloodshed and unrest throughout the entire Middle East. The proposal which the Royal Commission made in 1937 with regard to partition sufficed to provoke a national revolution which went on until the outbreak of the war. Moreover, in view of the country's geographical, economic and social conditions, no plan for partitioning can be feasible. This little country cannot be divided into two or three states which would feed only suspicion and hostility towards one another.

The only possible solution and the only one in the opinion of the Governments of the Arab States capable of settling the dispute would, as indicated in the draft submitted by the Arab delegation to the London Conference on Palestine in September 1946, be to form a free Government on the basis of proportional representation and to grant all the Jews who have acquired Palestinian nationality through legal channels the same rights as are recognized to Arab citizens. The Arabs who have always felt that the Jewish immigrants who had settled in Palestine since the beginning of the Mandate could not be considered Palestinian citizens, wish by these proposals to show proof of the conciliatory spirit by which they are motivated and their ardent desire to smooth out the difficulties.

The result of this arrangement could not, as certain Zionist leaders claim, be that the Jewish citizens of Palestine would fail to enjoy their full rights because of the fact that they would remain a minority. The Jewish minority in the Arab countries have never been maltreated. On the contrary, they live in perfect harmony with the majority and enjoy equal rights. From earliest times, the Arabs have never practised any discrimination between their citizens as regards race or religion, and to the Jewish community in particular they have always shown fair treatment based on the principles of justice and equality. Far from oppressing them, they have offered a refuge to those fleeing from persecution in other countries and some of them, benefiting by their recognized rights to liberty and equality have even attained the highest positions in the world of politics, administration, finance and science.

The Zionists try to justify their claims by saying that they wish to save their fellow Jews from the persecution to which they are at present subjected. Nevertheless, thanks to the victory or the democracies, there is no longer any hotbed of anti-Semitism anywhere in the world. The minorities have regained their full rights and are exercising them everywhere.

As far as the problem of refugees and displaced persons is concerned, it should be dealt with apart from the Palestine problem and settled on the basis of international cooperation and solidarity. There cannot be any question of transferring these refugees to Palestine en masse. The alleviation of the sufferings of one nation must not and cannot be sought in the aggravation of the sufferings of another nation and in its annihilation.

The Governments of the Arab States could not bring this statement to a close without again expressing the hope that your Committee, taking into consideration the views we have expressed herein, will adopt the only just solution to the problem, viz., recognition of the sovereign independence of Palestine and immediate discontinuation of immigration, which threatens to change the face of the country. For any solution which does not take into account the atmosphere of Palestine, i.e., the attitude of the peoples and of the Governments of the Arab States, would be doomed to certain failure. Moreover, it would only increase the dangers which now exist and hold dire threats for the future.

SPECIAL COMMITTEE ON PALESTINE
VERBATIM RECORD OF THE THIRTY-EIGHTH MEETING
(PUBLIC)
Held at the Ministry of Foreign Affairs
Beirut, Lebanon
Tuesday, 22 July 1947

VII

CHAIRMAN [Emil Sandström, Sweden] (Interpretation from French): The first series of questions has been asked on the assumption that an Arab State would be established in Palestine, as suggested by the other Arab States. The first question is the following: What would be the fate of illegal Jewish immigrants and such immigrants as have not acquired Palestinian nationality? This question is asked in relation to page 16 of the memorandum which said that this Palestinian State would grant to all Jews who had acquired Palestinian nationality through legal means the same right, and so on.

Mr. Hamid FRANGIE (Lebanon) (Interpretation from French): The first way to answer this question would be to define exactly the term "illegal immigrants". The Arabs consider that all Jews who entered Palestine since the Balfour Declaration are illegal immigrants. However, the Mandatory Power gave Palestinian nationality to a number of those immigrants. They are citizens *de facto*. The term "illegal", as it is put in the question, seems to designate Jews who entered Palestine without the permission of the Mandatory Power. Those Jews should be submitted to the rules which are presently applied to Arab illegal immigrants and envisaging, particularly, their expulsion from the country. There is no reason to establish discrimination in their favour. As regards those who entered Palestine according to rules presently in force on immigration, but who have not acquired Palestinian nationality, their condition will be determined by the future independent government of Palestine. Those who fulfilled the required conditions for acquisition of nationality should be considered as citizens. The others will be considered as foreigners without any discrimination.

CHAIRMAN (Interpretation from French): Does some other representative of the Arab States wish to give a special answer to that question?

Mr. Hamid FRANGIE (Lebanon) (Interpretation from French): What I am reading now has been decided on amongst the various States. There should be no individual replies to the questions.

Sir Abdur RAHMAN (India): Are they all agreed on this answer?

Mr. Hamid FRANGIE (Lebanon) (Interpretation from French): Yes.

Mr. LISICKY (Czechoslovakia) (Interpretation from French): Considering the definition we have been given of an "illegal immigrant", I would like to ask who, according to the views of the Arab representatives, is a legal immigrant in Palestine since the Balfour Declaration?

Emir Adel ARSLAN (Syria) (Interpretation from French): This would be the case: Legal immigrants would be foreigners who entered Palestine with the permission of the Mandatory Power which established from the very first a certain yearly proportion of immigrants. These we consider to be legal immigrants, since they fulfilled all the required conditions.

Mr. LISICKY (Czechoslovakia): I think there is a certain contradiction between what has just been said to us and the declaration which has been read by the Minister for Foreign Affairs, who said that in the mind of the Arab States any Jew who entered Palestine after the Balfour Declaration was an illegal immigrant, even those who have entered under the quota.

Emir Adel ARSLAN (Syria): The answer is that they were considered as citizens *de facto*.

CHAIRMAN (Interpretation from French): Who wishes to answer this question?

Emir Adel ARSLAN (Syria): I think there is no difficulty, Mr. Chairman. We consider those immigrants as citizens *de facto*, but we consider them as illegal because they entered Palestine after the Balfour Declaration, which we consider to be illegal.

Mr. LISICKY (Czechoslovakia) (Interpretation from French): Does this mean that if there had been no Balfour Declaration then all Jews could have entered Palestine legally? Is it only the fact that there exists this Balfour Declaration which makes any Jewish immigrant to Palestine an illegal immigrant?

Mr. Fadel JAMALI (Iraq): If there had been no Balfour Declaration there might have been one of two conditions. Either there would still have been an Ottoman Empire, whereby immigrants into the Ottoman Empire, of which Palestine was a part, would have had to submit to the laws of the Ottoman Empire; or, if there were no Ottoman Empire, there would have been an Arab State. Then the Arab State would have had its laws, and those who entered according to these laws would be legal immigrants, Jews or non-Jews.
...

CHAIRMAN (Interpretation from French): The second question is the following: On page 14 of the memorandum it is stated: "This proposal consists of the necessity of stopping immediately all Jewish immigration into Palestine, of maintaining the rules now in force on the transfer of the land." The question is: how does this harmonise with the principle of equal rights proclaimed on page 16? Another question on the same point is: Is the proposal on page 14 to be considered only as a temporary arrangement?

Mr. Hamid FRANGIE (Lebanon) (Interpretation from French): The Government of the Arab States wants the immediate stopping of immigration into Palestine and the prohibition of the transfer of land to Jews until a democratic independent state has been established in Palestine. When such a state has been established, then it will be able to make its own laws on the question.

…

CHAIRMAN (Interpretation from French): In your opinion, would the Jews have possibilities of developing freely in a Palestinian Arab State? Developing the question further: would they have the right of an educational system of their own; and further, what would happen to Jewish industry?

Mr. Hamid FRANGIE (Lebanon) (Interpretation from French): Our answer to the first part of this question is in the affirmative. In answer to the second part, the constitution of the independent State of Palestine will provide for the right of religious bodies and other societies and individuals to maintain, in addition to educational establishments administered by public authority, private schools and universities, subject to the compulsory teaching of Arabic in the schools and to Government control for the purpose of maintaining educational standards and preventing subversive teaching, with the object of creating common allegiance without discrimination among the citizens of the State. In answer to the third part of the question, Palestinian-Jewish industry will be treated as any other Palestinian industry and will be subject to the same laws.

...

CHAIRMAN (Interpretation from French): ... Question number five relates to the statement on page 16 of the memorandum, which says that the Jews in Arab States have never been badly treated, whereas the Jews contend that bad treatment had been inflicted on the Jews in one or two Arab States. What about this contradiction?

Mr. Hamid FRANGIE (Lebanon) (Interpretation from French): The Jews have always lived in peace in the Arab world and in perfect harmony with the other inhabitants of those countries. History shows many examples of the liberalism and tolerance of the Arabs toward all religions. It is to be attributed to Zionism that the relationship between Jews and non-Jews has been poisoned. The only incident which we can remember is the Nazi *coup d'état* in Baghdad in 1941, which was exploitation of the hostility of Arabs towards Zionism to incite violence by Arabs against Jews. But the legal Government of Iraq quickly put an end to this movement and punished those who were responsible for it very severely.

Sir Abdur RAHMAN (India): Shall I understand that it is the political aspirations which led to that trouble, and but for those political aspirations there would have been no trouble?

Mr. Fadel JAMALI (Iraq): The answer is in the affirmative, Sir. Were it not for Zionism, the atmosphere in the Arab world between the members of the various sects and religions would be very harmonious and peaceful. We in Iraq, before that Nazi *coup d'état*, never had any conflict between Jews and non-Jews. We consider Moslems, Christians and Jews as Arabs. We consider then all Arabs, all Iraqis. To us, Jews are only people who have a different faith, but they are part of us. We have nothing against them. They have lived, and they live today more prosperously than other sects and religions in Baghdad. There are great men in economics, finance and commerce in Iraq. So, the atmosphere is most cordial, were it not for Zionism. May I add one more word in this connection. We have Jews in parliament, in the Senate, in the highest posts in the Government. We even had a Cabinet member in Iraq who was a Jew.

...

Mr. Garcia GRANADOS (Guatemala) (Interpretation from French): I would like to return to the point of clarifying the causes of the troubles in Iraq. I think we came to an agreement that they were caused by the Nazi ideas which were at that time poisoning the minds of certain parts of the population there. Now, let us suppose that an Arab state is created in Palestine. Unfortunately, according to certain documents, and according to what was said by the Allies during the war, there are many members of the Arab Higher Committee who during the war had Nazi tendencies. Further, I think, from what I have seen in Palestine, that the members of the Arab Higher Committee are members of the most influential political party in Palestine, and therefore it is most likely that they would come into power. Do you not think that the same trouble might occur since we know that they had Nazi ideas during the war?

Mr. Hamid FRANGIE (Lebanon) (Interpretation from French): I think that to say the members of the Arab Higher Committee have Nazi ideas is an entirely unfounded accusation. First of all, the men who judged war criminals have not conceded that the members of the Arab Higher Committee are war criminals. The United Kingdom did not ask that the Mufti be extradited from Palestine as a war criminal. Secondly, if certain members of the Arab Higher Committee took refuge in Germany during the war it was not because they sympathized with the Nazi movement, but because they were fighting against the Jews and therefore they came to fight against Great Britain and could not find refuge anywhere but in Germany. After they left Palestine, the members of the Arab Higher Committee went, first of all, to friendly countries, such as Iraq, then to neutral countries, such as Iran, and finally when Iraq and Iran were occupied by the Allies, and particularly by the United Kingdom, they had to flee, and the only countries where they could take refuge were Italy and Germany. Further, I can state here very firmly that the Arab Higher Committee of Palestine was never at the service of any foreign power. Their only aim was to save Palestine from Zionism. We can also declare that the Arab Higher Committee, if it should take up the Government of Palestine, would certainly commit no acts of violence against the Jews. If we examine the present situation, we can see very clearly that the ideas of violence did not come from the Arab side, but that terrorism has been introduced and is being practised systematically by the Jews.

...

CHAIRMAN (Interpretation from French): ... For question number six we have in view the fact that the Mandatory Power found it necessary to have considerable armed forces to maintain order and peace in Palestine. Therefore, in the case of Palestine becoming an independent Arab State, how will law and order be maintained having in view the fact that the Mandatory Power needs considerable armed forces for that purpose under present circumstances?

Mr. Hamid FRANGIE (Lebanon) (Interpretation from French): The representatives of the Arab Governments consider that there should be created in Palestine an independent state with police forces sufficient to prevent any attempt at disorder from whatever side it would arise. The Governments are further convinced that if sufficient firmness is used it would not be necessary to have a very considerable number of police forces.

CHAIRMAN: (interpretation from French): You know as well as we do that certain disorders in Palestine now are caused by Jews and that the Jews have considerable underground forces, such as Haganah, and so on. Do you not think it would be necessary to have a rather strong police force to maintain order in that case?

Emir Adel ARSLAN (Syria) (Interpretation from French): We are convinced that the United Kingdom is maintaining large armed forces in Palestine but is not using those forces.

Mr. Hamid FRANGIE (Lebanon) (Interpretation from French): I said that we foresaw the necessity for such police forces, and if you wish to ask for details we could give you a study, as I think we could establish exactly what forces would be required. Up to now the United Kingdom has not taken very severe steps against the Underground. If I am correctly informed, there are official reports from the Government of Palestine saying that it would be possible to end those acts of terrorism within a comparatively short time; but up to now – probably in order not to shock public opinion in the world – they have not wanted to use reprisals against the Jews. I think the present troubles in Palestine have one aim; that is to excite the world in favour of the Jews. I think when the United Nations has said there should be an Arab State, and when that Arab State has been established in Palestine, the Jews will understand that they are doing their own cause more harm than good and they will try to come to an understanding in order to cooperate in that State.

CHAIRMAN (Interpretation from French): It was stated yesterday in the memorandum that the security of the Arab States would be jeopardized by the establishment of a Jewish State in Palestine. Do you consider that even if this State consisted of a small part of Palestine it would still constitute a danger? And how would security be threatened?

Mr. Hamid FRANGIE (Lebanon) (Interpretation from French): A Jewish State, however small, would constitute a danger for the Arab world both from the interior and the exterior. From the interior it would create friction, exert a certain economic pressure and would gradually infiltrate in order to create disorder. From the exterior, a Jewish State would constitute a bridgehead against the Arab world. Such is the collective answer of the delegations of the Arab States. I would like to add some words myself. I think that the question of the creation of a Jewish State cannot be taken without two other connected problems: that is, the question of immigration and that of foreign subsidies. A Jewish State would, of course, be master of the immigration into Palestine. It might decide that immigration would be without limits and the economic argument, which would be that it is impossible for a very large number of people to live in a very small territory, would become void if the Jewish State can still reckon with foreign financial support. Therefore, with the doors of the country wide open to immigration, and financial support from outside, the Jewish State would become extremely populated. Therefore, it might not be one million, but two, three, four million, since it would not depend on its own economy or its own production. As soon as it goes beyond a certain limit in numbers, it is no longer a State where Jews can come and be safe but it becomes a bridgehead against the Arab world. This is what we absolutely want to avoid. A Jewish State would not be accepted by the Jews if they had to put an end to immigration. Further, if they go on obtaining subsidies, this very highly populated country, enjoying foreign financial support, would certainly constitute a military danger for the Arab world.

Mr. Fouad HAMZA (Saudi Arabia): If you will permit me, I will simply add a few words. You may have the impression that the Arab States may be afraid of the establishment of a Jewish State in Palestine. This is not the case. The Arabs have never been afraid of the Jews and will never be afraid of them. What we are afraid of in the establishment of a Jewish State in Palestine is that it will create friction which will endanger the security of the whole of the Middle East. That is the most important problem. Taking into consideration the fact that Zionism is based on aggressive action, you know exactly what we may fear. In fact, we may also be afraid that any Jewish State, however small it may be, will be led by the terrorist elements whose acts you have seen.

Mr. Adel ARSLAN (Syria) (Interpretation from French): We must not forget that the question of establishing a Jewish State in Palestine is for the Arabs a question of national dignity. We shall never permit the creation of a Jewish State in Palestine. Otherwise, if any country would admit that a State may be created within its own national boundaries, it would not be necessary to send a committee, for instance, to the Balkans. There the dispute between Greece and Bulgaria is only a question of boundaries, of frontiers. But here in Palestine, it is not a problem simply of frontiers. Zionism wants to create a Jewish State within an Arab State. I do not think that any other country would admit such a thing.

Mr. ENTEZAM (Iran) (Interpretation from French): I would like to raise a question in connection with the explanation which has been given by the representative of Lebanon; that is to say, if I understand correctly, the danger which would be constituted by the creation of a Jewish State, however small, is that this Jewish State would be able to permit unlimited immigration, and reckoning with the financial support abroad, it would become exceedingly populated. Therefore, the problem of vital space would arise; that is to say, that this country might want to go beyond its own limits.

Mr. Hamid FRANGIE (Lebanon) (Interpretation from French): According to us, this is absolutely certain. It is only necessary to watch the requests of the Jews to see how they are growing. I recalled yesterday that the Jewish delegation to the Peace Conference did not dream of asking for the creation of a Jewish State. Every time the Jews obtain something, they establish themselves firmly upon what they obtain, and then want to ask for more. If I remember correctly, the Jewish National Home had been defined in 1919 by such responsible persons as Mr. Pichon from France: at the Peace Conference he said that it was to be a cultural national home. Lord Balfour also, the author of the famous Declaration, said something similar in 1922. At present it is no longer a question of a cultural home but a real national home, and the Jews demand the creation of a Jewish State in the whole of Palestine. Some go even further and say in the whole of historical Palestine, that is to say from Sinai to the Euphrates.

If, on the other hand, the idea is to have that Jewish State created on a smaller territory, then it is inevitable that it will become overpopulated and it will be impossible for that population to live on such a small territory. This would be certainly a reason for friction which the United Nations are trying to avoid. The United Nations are trying to avoid causes for new wars, but this might be a cause for a new war.

Mr. Fadel JAMALI (Iraq): I want to say what His Excellency the Lebanese Foreign Minister said. I will elaborate on the matter. To appreciate the danger to peace of a Jewish State in the Middle East, one has only to study the nature and history of Zionism, their method. They start with a small, very modest demand and then that grows bigger and bigger. They never first spoke of the Jewish State. I know very well that Dr. Weizmann acquiesced in the letter published in 1922 by the Colonial Office, saying their intention was not to have a Jewish State. I listened to Dr. Weizmann before the Anglo-American Committee last year when he stated that he always said "don't mention a Jewish State, the Jewish State will come." Now Dr. Weizmann is satisfied with partition, a small State, but that small State, part of Palestine, will ask for all of Palestine. But that is not enough. Transjordan would come. And that is not enough. Part of Southern Syria, Southern Lebanon, part of Egypt. And that is not enough. From the Nile to the Euphrates. That is what the terrorists say today. And even that is not enough. For the statements have appeared that they want actually the economic, if not political, penetration of the whole of the Middle East. We know these things. We are quite familiar with them. And history is proving and vindicating our views.

So, if that is not a cause of irritation and provocation, and if that is not a danger to peace, I do not know what could be a danger to peace and security in the Middle East. It is not that we are going to stand still or acquiesce or become passive. Not at all. But there is the danger. Struggle will be coming.

If you will permit me, I would like to give one very interesting example: A very modest and wise Jew who always preaches unity with the Arabs, Dr. Magnes. I have watched with great interest the gradual development of Dr. Magnes' views. I used to read his writings in 1929-1930. Then Dr. Magnes was against immigration, against any political intentions. He simply wanted a spiritual home in Palestine. That is all. The Jews did not want anything more than that. Later on, Dr. Magnes, in 1936, when the Arabs were revolting, said: "Why not let us come to a final understanding; let us agree that the Jews will never exceed forty per cent and the Arabs sixty per cent." Later on, more recently, he has come to the idea of parity, numerical parity. "That will settle the question", he says. But this is not the end. He says later on the Arabs may acquiesce that that parity may also be exceeded. And there we are. This is the most modest and the most peaceful Jew whom we see. Watch his growth, the growth of his demands. I do not know after parity has succeeded what official program of the Zionists will follow.

Emir Adel ARSLAN (Syria) (Interpretation from French): In 1922 I had the great advantage of travelling with Lord Milner, who drafted the Balfour Declaration. He declared there was only one member of the Cabinet of Great Britain at that time who refused to accept the Balfour Declaration, and that was Montague, a Jew. When he was asked for the reasons for his refusal, he said: "I think that this Declaration will be a great evil for the Jews because I know the Jews much better than you do and I know that if they were given this Declaration, they could bring about a great danger and a great evil."

...

CHAIRMAN (Interpretation from French): We proceed now to question number 4. Several solutions have been mentioned: (a) A bi-national State with a limited immigration, (b) A federal State, comprising two or more part States, each having the power to determine whether or not immigration would take place, (c) Partition, involving establishment of two independent States which as a matter of course would be at liberty to decide on the immigration question. What are your reasons for disregarding these solutions?

Mr. Hamid FRANGIE (Lebanon) (Interpretation from French): The reasons we have for refusing certain solutions are as follows: We consider that the establishment of a new State, or the establishment of a bridgehead, would be incompatible with our own rights.

CHAIRMAN (Interpretation from French): Do you consider all those solutions as having the same number of disadvantages? I would like to know if you adopt a certain order in those solutions?

Mr. Hamid FRANGIE (Lebanon) (Interpretation from French): No. We all refused them because they all have the same disadvantages.

Sir Abdur RAHMAN (India): Now, gentlemen, just look at the situation we are confronted with. There are six hundred to seven hundred thousand Jews in Palestine, and there are twelve hundred thousand Arab Christians and Moslems. We have to find a solution. Would you, considering the Jews to be a nation and considering the Arabs to be another nation, discard the idea of a bi-national State? I am not talking of parity just now because the words in the question do not refer to parity or non-parity. I am saying that given twelve hundred thousand Arabs and six hundred to seven hundred thousand Jews, would you really not consider the formation of a Government composed of these two peoples? I am leaving parity out of my question, for the time being. That is one part of the question. The other question that was involved is limited immigration. Now, immigration can be for two reasons: One political, and the other, religious. I am a Moslem, and some of you are Moslems. Suppose I, in my religious zeal, wish to come and visit Harem esh Sharif and wish to settle down, would you stop immigration altogether? I am saying that there are two aspects of immigration – political and religious. Your answer was in such general terms that I wish to stop and discuss with you in a little more detail as to what you are really trying to convey. Would you stop immigration even for the purpose of religious zeal if people wish to come to Palestine and wish to settle down there for that reason, whether they be Christian, Moslem or Jew? I am asking you that question, now. My question consists of two parts. Take both of them separately, please. Take first of all the creation of a State composed of two peoples – Jews, six or seven hundred thousand, and twelve hundred thousand Arabs. Now, we have been called upon to find a solution. Would you, without the question of parity being taken into consideration, discard the question of the composition of the Government composed of these two peoples in Palestine? The second question refers to immigration. Deal with them separately. I should like to have a little more detailed information from you on that point.

Emir Adel ARSLAN (Syria) (Interpretation from French): In the draft we presented in London to the British Government this question was studied very carefully; that is to say, the question of creating a State in Palestine where Jews would have a right to parliamentary representation and to positions in the Government. On the second part of the question there is a very important difference between immigration, immigrants, and visitors or pilgrims. It was stated yesterday, I think, and I repeat it, that access to Holy Places would be perfectly free. But on the other hand, if you suppose that a million Moslem individuals would like to come and settle in Palestine because they want to be near the Holy Places, then we would certainly refuse them. And since we would refuse that to Moslems who, after all, constitute the majority of the population, I see no reason why we should not deal with the Jews in the same way.

Mr. Camille CHAMOUN (Minister for the Interior of the Lebanese Republic) (Interpretation from French): As has been said before, this question has been studied very carefully at London during the Conference that took place on Palestine. If I understand the representative of India correctly, his question has two objectives. First of all, is there any possibility of establishing a unitary state in Palestine where Arabs and Jews would take part in the Government? And secondly, there is the question of full limitation of immigration.

On the first point, which was dealt with in detail in London, we insisted upon the safeguarding of the Arab character of Palestine, and within the framework of the Arab character we proposed that Jews, proportionately to their number in the country and the number who acquired Palestinian nationality should be asked to cooperate in the Government of the country. There should be called a constituent assembly composed, proportionately again, of Arabs and Jews who would define the constitution of Palestine. The result of this assembly would be the setting up of a Government composed of Arabs and Jews proportionately. Further, Jews and Arabs would also be represented proportionately in Parliament; all this in order to bring about the fullest possible cooperation between the two elements of the population. On this point I think we can give a satisfactory answer to the question put by the representative of India. We are not opposed to a reasonable solution through the creation of a State where Arabs and Jews would be proportionately represented, and further, we were the first to propose that Jews should be asked to cooperate in the Government of a new Palestinian State.

Beyond those proposals of a political character we proposed certain guarantees of a religious and cultural character, and further that certain special courts should be established for the Jews to solve certain questions of personal status. Our opinions given in London were perfectly constructive and certainly in accordance with the principles of the United Nations and in conformity with the Charter which aims at the maintenance of unity in Palestine. This is my answer to the first question.

Now for the second question. We were of the opinion, during that Conference on Palestine, and also here, that it is the affair of the future Government of Palestine to take any decisions about immigration. Up to now immigration has been only one way; that is to say, it has been only Jews who have immigrated into Palestine, and no Arabs at all. There have been cases where Arabs who wanted to immigrate into Palestine have been refused permission. Zionist immigration, therefore, has been one way and with only one aim, and that is to dominate Palestine. Therefore it is quite understandable that we want to be extremely circumspect and careful with regard to immigration and to regard it as the affair of the future Government of Palestine to decide upon this moot point. We certainly do not think the doors of the country should be closed, but there should be a certain definite control. Other countries control immigration. Why do such large countries as the United States, Brazil, Canada, and Australia impose certain limitations to immigration? It is to preserve their own national unity. Therefore, it is all the more important, in the case of a small country like Palestine. Immigration must be controlled and I think it is the duty and the full right of the future Government of Palestine to refuse entry into the country to certain subversive characters who would have a political opinion which might do harm to the country. I believe there will certainly be immigration in the new State, but it will be limited by the laws then existing in the country.

SPECIAL COMMITTEE ON PALESTINE
VERBATIM RECORD OF THE THIRTY-NINTH MEETING
(PRIVATE)
Held at the Grand Hotel, Sofar, Lebanon
Wednesday, 23 July 1947

VIII

Mr. Fadel JAMALI (Iraq): I have the honour on behalf of the Iraqi Government to subscribe to all that has been included in the memorandum submitted by the Arab States and beg permission to emphasize and to elaborate some of its points in this additional statement. My statement consists of four headings:
1. Arabs' right and aspirations and the Palestine Mandate
2. Zionist aims, claims, and methods
3. What is involved in the Palestine issue
4. Conclusions and proposals

(1) <u>Arabs' rights and aspirations and the Palestine Mandate</u>
Palestine is an integral part of the Arab world, and it is a vital part thereof. Geographically it is in the heart of the Arab world. To travel on the normal routes from north to south or from east to west of the Arab world one has to cross Palestine. Thus a traveller to Egypt from Iraq, or Syria, or Lebanon, or a traveller from Lebanon or Syria into Saudi Arabia and Hejaz for pilgrimage passes through Palestine. Palestine is only the southern part of the whole of natural and historical Syria. Nationally the indigenous people of Palestine are one and the same people as those of Syria, and culturally and nationally united with the rest of the Arab world.

The Arabs joined the Allies in World War I under the leadership of His late Majesty King Hussein and his sons (of whom King Feisal the First, the founder of the modern state of Iraq, was one) and fought for the liberation and unity of the Arabs, including the Arabs of Palestine. The Allies on their part made clear promises to the Arabs that they would support the Arabs in the attainment of their nationalistic aims, and they declared that their armies were coming to liberate and not to conquer the Arab lands, and it was taken for granted that the principle of self-determination would be applied to the liberated territories including Palestine. Palestine was no exception to the areas which were promised freedom and independence. But even without these promises are not the inhabitants of Palestine like the rest of the Arab world entitled to freedom and independence in their own home? The Arabs of Palestine, like the people of the rest of the Arab world, were hoping to attain their national aspirations. What was the result? The result was a great frustration and disappointment towards the end of World War I for in 1917 the Balfour Declaration was issued promising the Jews a Jewish national home in Palestine without the knowledge or consent of the indigenous inhabitants of Palestine, a great violation of all moral and human rights, and this is the root of all the trouble. When the Declaration was made, one of three assumptions must have been made: Either that Palestine was an empty country, a sort of no-man's land; or that the inhabitants of Palestine represented an enemy population whose territory could be dealt with at will; or that Palestine was inhabited by a people whose territory could be colonized and exploited without recognizing their right to say anything. All and each of these assumptions are wrong for Palestine is not a land without a people to be given to a people without a land. It has its own indigenous population, the inhabitants of Palestine. Many of its men took part in the Arab revolt in World War I on the side of the Allies and therefore they were entitled to their right to freedom and independence as friendly allies and not as enemies whose country could be disposed of without their knowledge or consent. Finally the people of Palestine, together with the people of the rest of the Arab World, are a people of great history and nature. They are not of the type to submit to foreign domination and colonization. The fact that some alien dreamers formed designs to come and occupy Palestine cannot be regarded but as a move of aggression and a violation of the principles of peace, justice and democracy.

Unfortunately, the Balfour Declaration was included in a Mandate designed by the League of Nations giving it an apparent international character. But this was a glaring mistake of the League of Nations. It was a move by the League of Nations that led to the violation of world peace and stability in this part of the world for the last 30 years. The Mandate violated in general all the principles of democracy and self-determination which were contained in the Covenant of the League of Nations. In particular, it violated the very spirit and letter of Paragraph 4, Article 22 of the Covenant of the League of Nations which reads as follows:

"Certain communities formerly belonging to the Turkish Empire have reached a stage of development where their existence as independent nations can be provisionally recognized, subject to the rendering of administrative advice and assistance by a Mandatory until such time as they are able to stand alone. The wishes of these communities was to be a principal consideration in the selection of a Mandatory."

This paragraph of Article 22 of the Covenant clearly recognizes the right of the Arabs of Palestine to independence and to the choice of the Mandatory power by the inhabitants. These rights the Mandate for Palestine ignored, just as it ignored the real object of the Mandate, that of holding people as a trust with the object of helping them toward self-government and independence and not with the object of imposing an alien body whose object is to dominate the country and establish a state therein. Thus we find that the Mandate over Palestine has no moral or legal foundations for the League of Nations had no legal or moral authority to violate the letter and spirit of its own Covenant.

What was the result? As was to be expected the Arabs from the very beginning never recognized the legality or the validity of the Mandate over Palestine. The day of the Balfour Declaration is a day of strikes and demonstrations every year throughout the Arab world. The Arabs of Palestine never stopped to resist or to protest against the imposition of the terms of the Mandate. Palestine turned into a land of struggles, strife and bloodshed instead of being a land of peace and harmony, and very naturally so, for no self-respecting people in the world can permit in any circumstances aliens to be introduced into their country by force and with the intention of dominating it while they have no say in the destiny of their own country.

The Arabs of Palestine resisted and revolted on several occasions in self-defence and the situation today is no better than what it was 30 years ago. The Arabs today, not only in Palestine but throughout the Arab world, are in a state of tension over the issue of Palestine.

They are all convinced that it is not right or just that the Arabs of Palestine should have been deprived of their rights to self-government and self-determination. It is not right that the independence of the country should have been withheld while surrounding Arab States like Iraq, Syria, Lebanon, and Trans-Jordan, which were in the same category as Palestine and were all integral parts of the Ottoman Empire, have attained their independence. The Arabs of Palestine are as well developed as the Arabs of these States which have achieved independence. The wishes of the inhabitants of Palestine for independence and their rejection of Zionist penetration were formally expressed to the same King-Crane Commission appointed by the late President Wilson as early as 1919.

We in Iraq are directly concerned with the problem of Palestine not only because we are bound with the Arabs of Palestine by all the bonds that go to make one nation, but also because Palestine is so situated geographically as to be of vital importance to Iraq economically and strategically. Besides we have about 150,000 Jews in Iraq whose interest and welfare are bound up with the interest and welfare of our country as a whole. In Iraq, Moslems, Christians, and Jews have lived happily together for centuries. Zionism, however, may poison the atmosphere of harmony between Iraqi Jews and their non-Jewish brethren, and we have to see to it in Iraq that Zionism does not disturb the good relationship prevailing between all the citizens of Iraq. As evidence of the importance we attach to Palestine this is the platform of our present Cabinet. Paragraph 3 reads as follows:

"Since Iraq considers the cause of Palestine to be its own cause the Government will endeavor by all means under its disposal to safeguard this part of the Arab World from the dangers besetting it."

(2) Zionist Aims, Claims and Methods

Right from the promulgation of the Balfour Declaration the Arabs expressed their apprehension and repugnance to Zionist demands. The Mandatory Power did its utmost to allay Arab fears of Zionist intentions, but time and experience justified Arab fears and apprehensions. The Zionists, coming first with modest demands, began to unfold their ambitions from year to year. Official

Zionism today [stands] where the extremists stood 30 years ago – for a Jewish State in Palestine. The extremists today are not satisfied with Palestine alone. They want Trans-Jordan to be attached to Palestine to form one Jewish State immediately. This Jewish State might extend from the Nile to the Euphrates at a later stage and some pronouncements have appeared to the effect that Zionist ambitions do not fall short of the economic, if not political, penetration of the whole Middle East.

The Biltmore programme, which represents the original Zionist programme today, consists of turning Palestine into a Jewish Commonwealth, opening the gates of Palestine for unlimited Jewish immigration, vesting the Jewish Agency with the power of controlling immigration and upbuilding the country. Certainly this declaration shows that the Zionists have moved a long way beyond the Balfour Declaration and the terms of the Mandate. This is exactly what the Arabs had anticipated from the Mandate and the Balfour Declaration. The Mandatory Power insists that they never understood the Mandate to promise a Jewish State and had no such excessive Zionist demands and ambitions in mind. But there they are. I submit that there would be no problem in Palestine today were it not for Zionist ambition and Zionist aggression. These are the roots of all the trouble and unless the Zionists are definitely and finally told to abandon their political dream, there can be no peace in the Middle East. Palestine is being invaded today by armed illegal immigrants carried by ships. Terrorism is rampant. If this is not an act of aggression and an infringement of international peace we do not know what aggression is.

The Zionists have used many arguments to justify their intended domination of Palestine. The first is their historical connection with Palestine. This argument is not valid because historical connections with lands today inhabited by other peoples cannot justify movements in the world's population. If this were to be permitted, most of the countries of the earth should exchange populations. South American citizens of Spanish descent cannot return to Spain today without the permission of the Spanish Government nor are the citizens of the United States of America, Canada and New Zealand of English descent entitled to go back to England without the consent of the Government of the United Kingdom. The historical connections of these people are relatively modern and not two thousand years old. Even if this principle were accepted the Jews are not historically more entitled to Palestine than its present-day inhabitants. The Jews actually ruled part of Palestine not more than 240 years and they lived there not even eight hundred years, the length of time which the Arabs lived in Spain, without the Arabs claiming any right to it today. The Arabs of Palestine, on the other hand, are mainly descendants of people who lived in Palestine before the Jews went there and have actually been in Palestine for the last fourteen hundred years.

As for the continued spiritual connection of the Jews with Palestine: This argument does not entitle them to return to Palestine either, for spiritually Palestine is holy to the Christians, Moslems and Jews alike. There are more than five hundred million Christians in the world and some three hundred million Moslems, all of whom are as much spiritually interested in Palestine as are the Jews. There is no reason why Palestine should be claimed as Jewish because the Jews have spiritual connections with it. The fact is that spiritual connections with a place do not necessarily entail political connections. All the Moslems in the world have spiritual connections with Hedjaz, but politically Hedjaz belongs to its own inhabitants. Moreover, the Moslems, with their traditions of liberalism and religious toleration towards the people of the book, namely the Christians and the Jews, have demonstrated how harmoniously Christians and Moslems live together in Palestine with freedom of worship enjoyed by all. The Jews as such have enjoyed such freedom of worship and toleration under the Moslems and they shall continue to do so. But Zionism poisons the atmosphere. Zionism has turned Palestine from a place of peace and spiritual life for all mankind into a place of material strife, struggles and bloodshed.

Another claim of the Zionists is that the Arabs are backward, and that Zionists coming to Palestine help them materially and raise their standard of living. This is a very old imperialistic argument. It is the argument of the white man's burden, the fallacy of which is already exposed to the world. One aggression after another, one war after another, was waged on the strength of this argument and the world is sick of it. The truth is that this is an excuse for domination. The Arabs do not want that rise in their standard of living which leads to the loss of their own country and to the inflow of foreign elements who have come in to dominate it; the Arabs are not a backward race; they have a glorious historical record. They do not need the Zionists to bring them civilization and culture. They certainly do not welcome many of the things brought by the Zionists into Palestine in the name of civilization and culture. The Arabs want to develop in the modern world in their own way and from within for no real culture can be achieved by imposition or superficial imitation. The Arabs facing the modern world are hoping to achieve a new cultural synthesis which is completely consonant with their great philosophy and world mission, a culture [based] on a human brotherhood with no racial or religious discrimination or superiorities. Zionism, very much like Nazism, is based on racial and religious discrimination and cannot provide the culture which the modern Arab wants. It has already discriminated against Arab employment on so-called Jewish national land where no Arab can be employed. As for material development, the Arabs can develop better without Zionist intervention. We in Iraq are finding our own way towards material and cultural progress. No Zionists were needed to open a thousand elementary schools, send hundreds of students to European and American institutions, establish hundreds of hospitals and health centres in Iraq, and introduce great irrigation projects. We still have a long way to go, but we need no Zionists. Thus the Zionist argument of carrying the white man's burden in Palestine is totally rejected.

Another argument used by the Zionists is that the Arabs have vast areas of land and that the Jews are homeless and they need land. The first part of the argument can be easily dismissed, for no matter how vast a people's country might be it is their own right to decide whether they will accept any newcomers or not, and whom to accept.

The Arabs are not the only people who have vast areas. The United States, Canada, Australia, the countries of South America, all possess vast areas of land that need development, but no one speaks of imposing any immigration on these countries without their consent, and especially an immigration which has an alien political domination as its aim.

But the most important part of the argument is the question of homelessness. This is a very dangerous concept. Why should the Zionists assume that the Jews are homeless? I submit that the home of every Jew is the country in which he is a citizen. The home of the Iraq Jew is Iraq, and I should hate to think that he felt homeless in Iraq. The home of the English Jew is England, and the home of the French Jew is France and of the Czechoslovak Jew, Czechoslovakia. There should be no Jewish homelessness and by spreading this concept Zionism is rendering a great disservice to Jews all over the world...

Here are some of the powerful means used by the Zionists to make their ambitions and aggressive intentions appear to be right. First, economic pressure. Zionists use great economic pressure to make the Arab sell his land. They allure him and they weaken him by offering an exorbitant sum of money for his land. The weak Arab succumbs and soon finds himself a landless, homeless fellow. Economic pressure is used in gaining support and in averting attacks.

We know of some well-known non-Jewish men who have been employed by Zionists and paid large sums of money to promote their cause. We also know of anti-Zionist people who cannot raise their voices fearing Zionist economic threats and boycotts. But money and economic pressure cannot make wrong right. With money goes political influence. In some countries Zionists have direct access to influential public men. With pressure of influence, with business partnership, the Zionists gain supporters in many countries. Such support cannot make what is wrong right and what is unjust just.

Probably the most effective means which they have used to attain their goal is propaganda. The Zionists have a well-organized machinery of propaganda with which the Arabs cannot possibly compete today. They have access to the press in most of the Western countries, besides providing their own press. Through the press Zionists try to prove their wrong right, and the right of the Arabs wrong. They usually follow three lines of propaganda: One is that there is nothing in the way of their achieving their own aims except the Nazi effendis and feudal lords; the masses of the Arabs do not mind Zionist domination and flourish under it. To this line of propaganda I need [to] add a word. You need only travel round the Arab world to discover for yourself whether it is only the effendis who are opposed to Zionism. I wish to assure you here that since the days of the Prophet Mohammed – may Prayer and Peace bless his soul – until today the Arabs have never been united on anything as they are in their unity to oppose Zionism. This is true not only of the Palestinian Arabs, but also of the Arabs throughout the Arab world.

I have just [now] a new book by a Dutch writer, Dr. Van der Neulen. It is called "Aden and the Hadhramut", a journey to Southern Arabia. I will read one paragraph to show you how these Arabs feel about Palestine: "Palestine policy had to contend with some fundamental errors, the bitter truth of which we saw in these far Arab lands. The distrust that had arisen would only disappear with the passing of time and the implementation of a wise policy of justice to the original Arab inhabitants of Palestine. When we talked to the Arabs we found it possible, while acknowledging their acquired and ancient rights, to stress the desirability of cooperation with the Jews, that might be profitable to both parties, and to point to the wonderful benefits which Jewish immigration to Palestine had already produced. From the discussions of political difficulties in that country, so rich in Jewish, Christian and Moslem tradition, I found it possible to state that these errors have had repercussions in the most distant tribal Arab countries which show that even the Bedouin in far distant lands are interested in the question of Palestine."

The second line of propaganda is that of Displaced Persons Camps. The question of displaced persons is a humanitarian matter which the Zionists try to exploit for their own political ends. The question of displaced persons should be settled on an international level, and the United Nations has already created a special organization to deal with the matter. This problem should not complicate the situation in Palestine arising from the Zionist struggle for political domination. To assist Zionist political domination in Palestine with the pretext of displaced persons is to create trouble in the Arab world. This is an anti-humanitarian act. One should not attempt to remove an injustice by committing a greater injustice.

The third line of Zionist propaganda is that of boasting of their own achievements in Palestine – sandy deserts turned into paradise, modern farms established, many factories erected, huge hospitals built, etc., etc. To this line of propaganda we have two observations to make. The first is that given an unlimited source of dollars from the Zionists in the United States and Western science and technique, any amount of construction and development could be done by anyone. The Arabs are doing their utmost with the limited resources at hand to work their own development. The second remark is that the Zionists fail to speak of the great losses incurred in what they have achieved. It is now a known fact that Zionist economy in Palestine is not self-supplied. It is running on a deficit of something like 40 percent paid from donations. But, one might ask, are the Zionists fools. Why should they take such risk? The answer is quite. The Zionists have not come only for Palestine, which is mainly a barren, rocky and sandy country.

Palestine is just a stepping-stone to the economic exploitation of the whole Middle East. In the long run, the Zionists dream of big economic returns which will make up for the temporary losses. Hence, the whole world needs critically to examine Zionist propaganda and Zionist influence on the world press if we are to achieve peace in a democratic world. Great donations of money in a humanitarian guise for terrorism and the aggressive invasion of Palestine must stop if we are to achieve peace in this part of the world.

A new method used by extreme Zionists in post-war years has been a resort to force. Some Zionists in this War probably joined the Allied Forces with a double end in view – the defeat of Hitler and the conquest of Palestine by force. They certainly learned some of the deadliest and most treacherous Nazi methods of warfare. They are applying them in Palestine today.

These are some of the Zionist methods by which they wish to dominate Palestine but the fact remains that it would have been better for all concerned if the Zionists came with a direct force for the invasion of Palestine as the Crusaders did in the past. These round-about methods and these false pretences and camouflaged tactics cannot serve the purpose of peace. The undisputed truth is that the Arabs are unanimously opposed to political Zionism and that the Zionists can never establish a State in the Arab world. Such an attempt is doomed for it is unnatural to graft a foreign state on the Arab.

[3] What is involved in the Palestine issue?

What is involved in the Palestine issue is whether the principles of peace and justice can prevail or whether domination by the force of money, distorted propaganda, political pressure and terrorism will succeed.

What is involved is the loyalty of the Jews in every city in the world – are they to be uprooted or helped to live in a free democratic world?

What is involved is the future of the United Nations and the maintenance of the principles of the Charter, for the illegal immigrants invade Palestine and the terrorists practise violence under the very eyes of the United Nations Committee.

What is involved is the relationship between East and West for the East looks at Zionism as a Western desire inspired by old imperialistic methods which showed no respect for the rights and wishes of the people of the exploited country.

What is involved is the spiritual serenity of Palestine – whether it is to be a cradle of peace and holiness where the spirit of man can find a refuge, or a place where struggle and bloodshed between peoples of different religions and races prevail.

Much is involved in the question of Palestine and yet the question is so simple and the remedy is easy to apply. It is simple in spite of Zionist claims and propaganda which have created a complex problem out of a simple matter of invasion and desire for domination. It is easy in spite of terrorist violence for we believe that terrorism could easily be squashed with firmer handling of the situation.

[4] In conclusion, may I summarize my views and recommendations in the following:

Palestine is an integral part of the Arab world and the Arab population are the rightful owners of the country, and the Arabs will never yield Palestine or any part thereof. There is nothing between Arabs and Jews; as such they can live together harmoniously as they have done for thousands of years past.

The Mandate has no moral or legal foundation; it has introduced an element of trouble in Palestine which will continue to grow from year to year and disturb peace and stability throughout the Middle East unless the United Nations checks the source of trouble finally and completely.

The source of trouble is political Zionism with its ever-growing ambitions. Unless these political ambitions are finally and completely abandoned there can be no peace in Palestine or the Middle East. This can be done very easily if the United Nations declares that Zionist political ambitions are dangerous to peace and security in the Middle East, for Arab nationalism and political Zionism cannot go well together in Palestine. Either one or the other must disappear. The Arabs being the rightful inhabitants in Palestine are not ready to give up their Arab nationalism which is directly connected with all the Arab world. They will sooner or later fight for their political existence and defend their own country if aggression is permitted to continue. The Zionists should be advised to content themselves with the cultural and spiritual home which they have already achieved and abandon their aggressive political designs.

The Zionists should all understand that a Jewish State was never promised and can never be established in the whole or part of Palestine. Such a State can never survive with hostile people surrounding it and will always be a cause of war and struggle. We do not believe that the Jews need a State for they belong to the States where they reside. If it is deemed that a Jewish State is a human necessity it should be dealt with outside Palestine where no trouble will ensue.

A unitary democratic state should be established in Palestine where the people of Palestine, irrespective of race and religion, shall work together and live together peacefully and in harmony. Those who do not wish to live in such a State should be advised to leave Palestine.

Some Zionists who want a Jewish State, no matter how small to begin with, and some non-Jews who are not familiar with the situation, speak of partition as a solution. I wish to make it clear that no partition in any form or guise will be acceptable to the Arabs. They will fight it and resist sooner or later for no Jewish State in any size or form will ever be tolerated by the Arab world. Moreover, partition cannot work for more than one reason for it can never separate the Arabs from the Jews completely, and the State derived therefrom can never stand on its own feet economically. But these are from the Arab point of view, secondary considerations compared with their firm determination to fight the idea of partition as well as the idea of the Jewish State. I hope the Committee will give due consideration to this point.

Palestine is already relatively over-crowded if due consideration were given to the barrenness of the country and the natural growth of the population. That is why immigration should be completely stopped. If immigration ever were possible it should not take place without the consent of the Arabs of Palestine and their view of the absorptive capacity of the country should be paramount. Even then immigration should not be discriminatory and there is no justification for having

Jewish immigrants mainly. The quota should be fairly distributed amongst all Moslems, Christians and Jews who wish to come to Palestine to lead a spiritual life.

An independent democratic Palestine shall be recognized by the Members of the United Nations, and as such it shall be a Member of the Arab League and of the United Nations.

An experience of thirty years proved that flagrant injustice was done to the political rights of the Arabs of Palestine. That injustice led to strife and unrest throughout this period. Many committees and commissions were sent and made reports, with no avail. The Arabs have become desperate and they have lost hope in committees. May this Committee at last, guided by the principles of the Charter, make such recommendations which will finally remove the source of trouble and injustice, bring about clarity and finality in the situation so that peace and harmony may prevail in the Land of Peace and in all the Middle East.

…

Mr. Fouad HAMZA (Saudi Arabia): … The Saudi Arabian Government, who stands by the side of the sister Arab States and the Arabs of Palestine, wishes to explain a few outstanding points as to what is being thought by the Arabs in their different countries.

Never in the history of human conflicts have any people or country suffered an injustice so grave as the injustice and calamities suffered by the Arabs of Palestine. They have always been a peace-loving nation against whom force and aggression have been directed, with a view not only of imposing the rule of a foreign regime, but of a foreign and alien people upon their country; an alien people aiming at ousting the Arabs from their homeland or at best imposing their domination and rule upon them. The extent of Arab suffering and bitterness is not to be minimised.

The members of your honourable Committee represent free and democratic nations of whom some have tasted foreign rule and struggled through long years to retrieve their lost liberty and independence. You can therefore best appreciate our position. We have no doubt that the members of this honourable committee will conduct their investigations as best meets with the dictates of conscience, and that every effort will be made to find a lasting settlement which will remove the cause of injustice.

Might we here remark that any effort to assist persecuted people cannot be sincere if such assistance is to be at the cost and detriment of others. Consequently the world refugee problem must be treated on its own merits and not in relation to Palestine. It should in our opinion be kept distinct and separate and not serve as justification or cause for dispossessing the Arab people of Palestine of their rightful heritage, and replacing their corporate and national structure with an artificially created entity.

Zionism has no rightful claim on Palestine. In the implementation of their programme, they have exclusively relied on the support of a foreign power regime conducting itself arbitrarily and unjustly. Their forces have been forces of repression.

Zionists claim that foreign rule in Palestine and the influx of Jews into the country with their capital have contributed to the raising of the standard of living of the Arabs of Palestine. These allegations cannot bear the test of objective scrutiny. The whole of the administrative machinery of the Government of Palestine had been geared chiefly to facilitate the establishment of a Jewish National home and not for the promotion and development of the Arabs. In this respect nearly half the total budget of the Palestine Government is spent on maintaining non-existing security. What the Arabs, given a chance to develop peacefully and normally, are capable of doing can be evidenced in the Arab neighbouring countries. That in itself is a refutation of Zionist allegations. In fact we go as far as to assert that Zionism has been a direct cause of the retardation of Arab development in Palestine: given a chance to develop under favourable conditions they would have travelled far on the road of progress. Even if the Zionist allegation were held to be true, it should not serve as a basis or a pretext for dispossessing the Arabs of their own country.

We have full confidence in this honourable Committee. We are firmly convinced of the justice of the Arab case. Our belief is strong in the desire of the United Nations to carry out a just course in the interests of peace and security in this part of the world.

Thus in resting our case upon your sense of justice we sincerely hope for the establishment of permanent peace. You will thereby have rendered service to a just cause in the interests of humanity. You will have rendered service to the Arabs who will long remain.

SPECIAL COMMITTEE ON PALESTINE
VERBATIM RECORD OF THE THIRTY-NINTH MEETING
(PRIVATE)
Held at the Grand Hotel, Sofar, Lebanon
Wednesday, 23 July 1947

IX

SPECIAL NOTE BY SIR ABDUR RAHMAN, REPRESENTATIVE OF INDIA

(I) INDEPENDENCE OF PALESTINE

Independence is the natural birthright of every people of the world. This principle was given specific recognition before the First World War had come to an end. In his address of 4 July 1918, President Wilson laid down the following as one of the four great "ends for which the associated people of the world were fighting":

"The settlement of every question, whether of territory, of sovereignty, of economic arrangement or of political relations upon the basis of the free acceptance of that settlement by the people immediately concerned, and not upon the basis of the material interest or advantage of any other nation or people which may desire a different settlement for the sake of its own exterior influence or mastery."

If the right of self-determination of peoples, as envisaged by President Wilson (and on which the first four paragraphs of Article 22 of the Covenant of the League of Nations were based) is to be the determining factor and if imperialistic designs are to be countenanced no longer, there is no escape from the conclusion that Independence should be granted to Palestine forthwith, subject to such interim arrangements for the transfer of power as may seem to be desirable.

The people of Palestine have now admittedly reached a stage of development where their recognition as an independent nation can no longer be delayed. They are in no way less advanced than the people of the other free and independent Asiatic countries. It was admitted by Mr. Bevin, British Foreign Secretary, on 25 February 1947, that the cultural development of Arabs and Jews in Palestine was of as high a standard as in any other Arab State; and when we find that the other Arab States of the Middle East which had been placed under mandates have already acquired self-government, there appears to be no reason why this should any longer be withheld from the people of Palestine.

The provisions of the Mandate for Palestine are themselves based on Article 22 of the Covenant of the League of Nations. Indeed, the principle that independence for the population of Palestine should be the purpose of any plan, though not specifically included in the terms of reference of this Committee, found general acceptance at the special session of the General Assembly which brought the Committee into being. This was obviously so, since one of the purposes of the United Nations was, according to Article I of the Charter, "to develop friendly relations among nations based on respect for the principle of equal rights and self-determination of peoples" and the obligations of the United Nations under the present Charter were to prevail "in the event of a conflict between the obligations of the Members of the United Nations under the present Charter and their obligations under any other international agreement".

There can be no manner of doubt that King Hussein and the Arabs regarded these statements as containing an unqualified promise of independence to all Arab countries, including Palestine, as soon as Turkey was defeated. This conclusion can be fully substantiated not only by the terms of the letters as they had been conveyed to King Hussein, but also by declarations made on behalf of the British Government on several occasions. One can easily visualize what would have happened if the Arabs had been told at the time that Palestine was not to receive independence along with other Arab countries.

1. A communication was sent by the Acting British Agent at Jeddah, Mr. J. B. Bassett, on behalf of the British Government, to the King of Hejaz on 8 February 1918. To appreciate this letter, it might be mentioned that King Hussein had heard through Turkish sources that the British Government had entered into a pact with Russia and France in regard to the division of Arab territories (Sykes-Picot agreement). His suspicions, aroused in view of what had been considered by him to have been agreed, were quelled by the following words, where again the assurances of the liberation of the Arab peoples were reiterated:

"It would be superfluous to point out that the object aimed at by Turkey is to sow doubt and suspicion between the Allied Powers and those Arabs who, under Your Majesty's leadership and guidance, are striving nobly to recover their ancient freedom. The Turkish policy is to create dissension by luring the Arabs into believing that the Allied Powers have designs on the Arab countries, and by representing to the Allies that the Arabs might be made to renounce their aspirations. But such intrigues cannot succeed in sowing dissension among those whose minds are directed by a common purpose to a common end.

"His Majesty's Government and their Allies stand steadfastly by every cause aiming at the liberation of the oppressed nations, and they are determined to stand by the Arab peoples in their struggle for the establishment of an Arab world in which law shall replace Ottoman injustice, and in which unity shall prevail over the rivalries artificially provoked by the policy of Turkish officials. His Majesty's Government reaffirm their former pledge in regard to the liberation of the Arab peoples. His Majesty's Government have hitherto made it their policy to ensure that liberation, and it remains the policy they are determined unflinchingly to pursue by protecting such Arabs as are already liberated from all dangers and perils, and by assisting those who are still under the yoke of the tyrants to obtain their freedom."

2. This was followed by the British Government "Declaration to the Seven" (Arabs) on 16 June 1918 (Command 5964). It reads:

"His Majesty's Government have considered the memorial of the seven with the greatest care. His Majesty's Government fully appreciates the reasons why the memorialists desire to retain their anonymity, and the fact that the memorial is anonymous has not in any way detracted from the importance which His Majesty's Government eminent attribute to the document. The areas mentioned in the memorandum fall into four categories:

"1. Areas in Arabia which were free and independent before the outbreak of war;
"2. Areas emancipated from Turkish control by the action of the Arabs themselves during the present war;
"3. Areas formerly under Ottoman dominion, occupied by the Allied forces during the present war;
"4. Areas still under Turkish control.

"In regard to the first two categories, His Majesty's Government recognize the complete and sovereign independence of the Arabs inhabiting those areas and support them in their struggle for freedom.

"In regard to the areas occupied by the Allied forces, His Majesty's Government draw the attention of the memorialists to the texts of the proclamations issued respectively by the General Officers Commanding-in-Chief on the taking of Baghdad and Jerusalem. These proclamations embody the policy of His Majesty's Government towards the inhabitants of those regions. It is the wish and desire of His Majesty's Government that the future government of those regions should be based upon the principle of the consent of the governed, and this policy has and will continue to have the support of His Majesty's Government.

"In regard to the areas mentioned in the fourth category, it is the wish and desire of His Majesty's Government that the oppressed peoples of those areas should obtain their freedom and independence, and towards the achievement of this object His Majesty's Government continue to labour.

"His Majesty's Government are fully aware of, and take into consideration, the difficulties and dangers which beset those who work for the regeneration of the populations of the areas specified.

"In spite, however, of those obstacles His Majesty's Government trust and believe that they can and will be overcome, and wish to give all support to those who desire to overcome them. They are prepared to consider any scheme of cooperation which is compatible with existing military operations and consistent with the political principles of His Majesty's Government and the Allies."

3. This was again followed (17 October 1918) by the general assurance given by General Sir Edmund Allenby, on the occasion of the evacuation of Beirut by the Sharifian forces, regarding occupied enemy territory:

"I gave the Amir Faisal an official assurance that, whatever measures might be taken during the period of military administration, they were purely provisional and could not be allowed to prejudice the final settlement by the peace conference, at which no doubt the Arabs would have a representative. I added that the instructions to the military governors would preclude their mixing in political affairs, and that I should remove them if I found any of them contravening these orders. I reminded the Amir Faisal that the Allies were in honour bound to endeavour to reach a settlement in accordance with the wishes of the peoples concerned, and urged him to place his trust wholeheartedly in their good faith."

4. The Anglo-French Declaration was issued in Palestine, Syria, and Iraq in the form of an official communiqué emanating from General Head-quarters, Egyptian Expeditionary Forces, on 7 November 1918:

"The goal envisaged by France and Great Britain in prosecuting in the East the war set in train by German ambition is the complete and final liberation of the peoples who have for so long been oppressed by the Turks, and the setting up of national governments and administrations that shall derive their authority from the free exercise of the initiative and choice of the indigenous populations.

"In pursuit of those intentions, France and Great Britain agree to further and assist in the setting up of indigenous governments and administrations in Syria and Mesopotamia, which have already been liberated by the Allies, as well as in those territories which they have been endeavouring to liberate, and to recognize them as soon as they are actually set up.

"Far from wishing to impose this or that system upon the populations of those regions, their [i.e., France's and Great Britain's] only concern is to offer such support and efficacious help as will ensure the smooth working of the governments and administrations which those populations will have elected of their own free will to have; to secure impartial and equal justice for all; to facilitate the economic development of the country by promoting and encouraging local initiative; to foster the spread of education; and to put an end to the dissensions which Turkish policy has for so long exploited. Such is the task which the two Allied Powers wish to undertake in the liberated territories."

5. The Treaty of Sevres' of 10 August 1920, by which the High Contracting Parties had agreed to recognize Syria and Mesopotamia as dependent States in accordance with Article 22 of the Covenant of the League of Nations, subject to the rendering of administrative advice by a mandatory until they were able to stand alone, was not confirmed. But article 16 of the Treaty of Lausanne, which was signed on 24 July 1923, reads as follows:

"Turkey hereby renounces all rights and title whatsoever over or respecting the territories situated outside the frontiers laid down in the present Treaty and the islands other than those over which her sovereignty is recognized by the said Treaty, the future of these territories and islands being settled or to be settled by the parties concerned.

"The provisions of the present article do not prejudice any special arrangements arising from neighbourly relations which have been or may be concluded between Turkey and any multiple countries." ...

For the above reasons, independence should be granted to Palestine forthwith. ...

(II) THE MANDATE AND BALFOUR DECLARATION IN THEIR HISTORICAL SETTING

It is now necessary to consider the contention advanced on behalf of the Arab States to the effect that the Mandate, being in conflict with the terms and spirit of Article 22 of the Covenant of the League of Nations, was invalid and should not have been granted by the League of Nations or enforced by the mandatory. In order to examine this contention, it would be desirable to consider the Balfour Declaration and the Mandate, however briefly, in their historical setting. The Mandate for Palestine was assigned to the United Kingdom by the Supreme Council of the Allied Powers at San Remo in April 1920. Its terms were approved by the Council of the League of Nations on 24 July 1922, although it could not be formally given effect until after the Treaty of Lausanne was brought into force towards the end of September 1923.

The real questions to decide are the following:
(a) Whether the Balfour Declaration, made on behalf of the United Kingdom in November 1917–before

Palestine had ceased to be a part of the Ottoman Empire–should have been made, for it cannot reasonably be disputed that the creation of the Mandate was procured by the United Kingdom in view of what was regarded to be an undertaking given by the United Kingdom to the Jews;

(b) Whether the Mandate was, as a matter of fact, in conflict or inconsistent with the Covenant of the League of Nations;

(c) In case there is found to be a conflict or inconsistency between the two, which of them is to prevail;

(d) Whether or not the Mandate is in conflict or inconsistent with the Covenant, what is the legal effect of the former on the action taken by the mandatory Power in regard to the administration of Palestine in general and as regards Jewish immigration into that country in particular?

The First World War started in August 1914, and Turkey was drawn into it shortly afterwards. There was a powerful Zionist element in existence at the time in Germany and Austria, which was actually in negotiation with the Central Powers for the granting of certain rights in Palestine, and thus was provided with an interest in an Entente victory. The United Kingdom must naturally have been anxious to win over this element, and the Zionist group, led by at least two influential persons–Baron Rothschild, a well-known figure in British political circles, and Dr. Weizmann, a highly distinguished scientist who was at the time working in the Ministry of War–lost no time in pressing the Zionist demand for Palestine. But Mr. Asquith, the Prime Minister of England at the time, was not at all sympathetic towards the suggestion and wrote in his diary on 28 January 1915:

"I have just received from Herbert Samuel a memorandum headed 'The Future of Palestine'. He goes on to argue at considerable length and with some vehemence in favour of the British annexation of Palestine, a country the size of Wales, much of it barren mountains and part of it waterless. He thinks we might plant in this not very promising territory about three or four million European Jews, and that this would have a good effect upon those who are left behind. It reads almost like a new edition of Tatler brought up to date. I confess I am not attracted by this proposed addition to our responsibilities. But it is a curious illustration of Dizzy's favourite maxim that 'race is everything' to find this almost lyrical outburst proceeding from the well-ordered and methodical brain of Herbert Samuel."

An entry in Mr. Asquith's diary dated 13 March 1915 reads as follows:

"...I have already referred to Herbert Samuel's dithyrambic memorandum, urging that in the carving of the Turks' Asiatic dominion we should take Palestine, into which the scattered Jews would in time swarm back from all quarters of the globe, and in due course obtain home rule. Curiously enough, the only other partisan of this proposal is Lloyd George who, I need not say, does not care a damn for the Jews or their past or their future, but thinks it will be an outrage to let the Holy Places pass into the possession or under the protectorate of 'agnostic, atheistic France'."

There was also a volume of Jewish opinion in Britain itself which was opposed to this demand—not on account of British interests, not on account of their personal interests (as Dr. Weizmann seemed to suggest in his evidence before the Committee), but in the interest of the Jews themselves. Jews of this opinion were opposed to the idea of political Zionism and its nationalistic implications, and were afraid of being treated as strangers in their own countries. That is why a statement appeared in *The Times* of 24 May 1917 over the signatures of Messrs. David Alexander, president of the Board of Deputies of British Jews, and Claude G. Montefiore, president of the Anglo-Jewish Association. In this statement, although they stressed their fidelity to cultural Zionism, the aim of which was to make Palestine a spiritual centre where Jewish genius might develop along its own line, they entered a strong protest against the idea of political Zionism, which claimed that the Jewish settlements in Palestine should be recognized as possessing a national character in a political sense, and that the settlers should be invested with certain special rights on a basis of political privileges and economic preferences. The signers of this statement prophesied that the establishment of a Jewish nationality in Palestine would be bound to "have the effect throughout the world of stamping the Jews as strangers in their native lands, and of undermining their hard-won position as citizens and nationals of these lands." This notion was fully supported by Mr. Edwin Montagu, the then Secretary of State for India.

At the same time, it was essential for Great Britain to mitigate the "hostility of Jews in Allied countries" towards Russia, and to give those Jews who had been so active in overthrowing the Czarist regime an incentive to keep Russia in the war. There was also an imperialistic motive, that of securing Palestine or a portion of it as a bulwark to the British position in Egypt and to protect the overland link to the East, including India. Sir Martin Conway, Member of Parliament and well-known British politician, wrote a book about Palestine and Morocco in 1922; in it he stated that the control of Egypt alone was not sufficient for protecting the Suez Canal:

"The real danger to the Canal does not in, fact come from the West, but from the East..., It must ever be from the side of Palestine that serious danger will come. Behind Palestine is Syria, behind Syria are the Turks and behind the Turks is any European Power that may be hostile to Great Britain-Germany in the past, Russia perhaps in the future, who can say? The French have proved more of rivals than friends... and therefore Great Britain's hold on Palestine is of imperial interest of the highest order."

These considerations, and the fact that the war had assumed a dangerous phase in 1917 and nobody could say for a certainty what the final result would be, must have led the British Government to change its policy. Mr. Asquith had gone and had been succeeded by Mr. Lloyd George who was, on account of the British policy, not willing to let France have sway over Palestine which was, because of the empire in the East, so important strategically. A defeat to the United Kingdom, moreover, would have meant its extinction and the supremacy of autocracies over democracies.

These were briefly, in my view, the reasons which had led to the Balfour Declaration. But its language was the subject of discussion for a long time between the Jews and the British Government. In England "many different versions of the suggested formula were drafted by various members of the Zionist Political Committee" (official Zionist report) on both sides of the Atlantic. This was admitted by Dr. Weizmann in his evidence. He was not in a position, however, to produce the draft or drafts. But when his attention was drawn to those printed by Jeffries in his book, *Palestine-The Reality*,

Dr. Weizmann admitted that the words "a National Home for the Jewish people in Palestine" had been substituted for the expression, used in the earlier drafts, of Palestine being a National Home for the Jewish people. Speaking in Wales in [1930], Mr. Lloyd George himself assured his hearers that the Declaration "was prepared after much consideration not merely of its policy but of its actual wording".

The amendment was significant, as the whole of Palestine was not recognized in the Declaration for the use of the National Home. Moreover, it would be seen from the words that no promise was being made to the Jews of the creation of a State or of attempting to make an Arab majority into a minority by any process of immigration or otherwise. Indeed, the Declaration clearly provided that "nothing shall be done which may prejudice the civil and religious rights of existing non-Jewish communities in Palestine". This was a very important reservation and it was apparently made on account of promises which had already been made to the Arabs, and to which I shall advert shortly.

But I must say that any suggestion by which the Arabs could be converted into a minority, or even much less by which they were to lose *a* part of their country, was not even contemplated. Their civil rights had been expressly saved. In fact, the suggestion made by Dr. Weizmann in his interview with *The Times* on 1 March 1918, that "By the establishment of a Jewish National Home we mean the creation of such conditions in Palestine as will enable us to move large numbers of Jews into the land ... so that the country may become as quickly as possible as Jewish as England is English" elicited a clear statement from Mr. Winston Churchill. In his statement of British policy in Palestine of 3 June 1922, Mr. Churchill declared that "Phrases have been used *such* as that Palestine is to become 'as Jewish as England is English'. His Majesty's Government regard any such expectations as impracticable and have no such aim in view." Moreover, the Declaration was at the outside the statement of a policy which the Government of the United Kingdom had agreed to pursue in the event it was victorious and was legally in a position to advance that policy. The United Kingdom did come out victorious, but whether it was legally or even morally bound to advance the policy is a different matter. This would largely depend upon the position of the United Kingdom at the time and on the commitments, if any, already entered into by it before the date of this Declaration.

The reasons which had led the Government of the United Kingdom to enter into an alliance with the Arabs have been given by me elsewhere, and need not be repeated. Suffice it to say that on a declaration of jihad by the Porte after Turkey had joined Germany, it was vital for the British Government to counteract that effort in *such* a manner as to avoid a Moslem uprising in its Empire.

That is why Sir John Maxwell, who was then commanding the British forces in Egypt, advised Lord Kitchener on 16 October 1914 in the following words: "I do not know what the policy of the Foreign Office is, but I think the Arabs about Mecca and the Yemen ought to be approached and set against the Turks."

Since King Hussein's son, Amir Abdullah (now King of Transjordan), had already written to Mr. Ronald Storrs on the subject, on 14 July 1915, Lord Kitchener telegraphed a reply to the British Agency in Cairo on 31 October to be despatched to Amir Abdullah. The terms of that letter were general, but it held out a promise of support to the Arabs for freedom, on condition that they ally themselves with England. In the meantime, Sharif Hussein's first note was written to Sir Henry McMahon on the same date on which his son Amir Abdullah wrote to Mr. Storrs, and in this letter it was clearly stated that the Arab nation had decided to approach the Government of Great Britain with a request for the approval, through one of its representatives, if it thought fit, of the following basic provisions:

"Great Britain recognizes the independence of the Arab countries which are bounded: on the north, by the line Mersin-Adana to parallel 37° N. and thence along the line Birejik-Urfa-Mardin-Midiat-Jazirat (ibn 'Umar) - Amadia to the Persian frontier; on the east, by the Persian frontier down to the Persian Gulf; on the south, by the Indian Ocean (with the exclusion of Aden whose status will remain as at present); on the west, by the Red Sea and the Mediterranean Sea back to Mersin."

Sir Henry McMahon's reply on 30 August 1915 was evasive, and the Sharif wrote a longer note on 9 September 1915. In this it was clearly pointed out that the demand in regard to the proposed frontiers and boundaries was fundamental, and that they represented "not the suggestions of one individual . . . but the demands of our people who believe that those frontiers form the minimum necessary to the establishment of the new order for which they are striving". The reply to this note was sent by Sir Henry McMahon on 24 October 1915, and since he had been informed of the actual Arab situation through other Arab sources, he was more explicit in that letter. He agreed that, with the exception of the districts of Mersina and Alexandretta and portions of Syria lying to the west of Damascus, Homs, Hama and Aleppo, "Great Britain is prepared to recognize and uphold the independence of the Arabs in all the regions lying within the frontiers proposed by the Sharif of Mecca."

Thus, it is clear that Great Britain had expressed her readiness to assist the Arabs unequivocally in the setting up of suitable administrative arrangements in the areas of Arab independence. The Sharif, in his reply of 5 November 1915, consented to the exclusion of the Vilayet of Adana from the area of Arab independence, but refused to accept the exclusion of portions of Syria lying to the west of Damascus, Homs, Hama and Aleppo. Nor did he admit the exclusion of Alexandretta. Sir Henry McMahon, in his reply of 13 December, expressed his satisfaction at the exclusion of the Vilayet of Adana, but maintained his reservation of the *coastal* regions of northern Syria, not on the plea advanced by him before that *they* were not purely Arab, but solely on the ground that French interests were involved. The Sharif, in his reply dated 1 January 1916, although anxious to avoid any conflict between France and Great Britain, gave clearly to understand that France or any other Power could not secure "a single square foot of territory in those parts", and that he would seize the earliest opportunity after the war to indicate the Arab claims to the whole of Syria. In his reply of 30 January 1916, Sir Henry merely indicated that, in the event that France maintained its claims, Great Britain could not hold out any guarantees that the portions which had been excepted from the Arab areas in the letter of 24 October would be included in the territories in which Great Britain had pledged itself to recognize and uphold Arab independence.

It is clear from these letters that Palestine was not specifically excluded from the areas in which Arab independence had been asked for and in which it was agreed that Arab independence would be granted.

Moreover, any map would show that Palestine lies to the south and not to the west of the districts of Damascus, Homs, Hama and Aleppo, which were specifically referred to in the correspondence to which reference has already been made. The vilayets of the province of Syria were those of Aleppo, Beirut and Syria. Deir-ez-Zor, Lebanon and Jerusalem were centrally administered sanjaqs or counties outside the vilayets. Lebanon had a special autonomous regime. There was no Vilayet of Damascus; it did not exist. That is why "District had been used in McMahon's text, "the Vilayet of Damascus" referred to by Mr. Churchill as Colonial Secretary was obviously incorrect. It must also be remembered that if McMahon had Palestine in mind, he would have certainly added "and the Sanjaq of Jerusalem" to the vilayets of Aleppo and Beirut.

There is thus no doubt in my mind that, from what was stated in the letters, the only possible conclusion can be that it was promised that independence would be granted to the present Palestine along with the other Arab countries. This promise can be supported by the other documents such as Bassett's letter, "Hogarth's message," the "Declaration to the Seven," and the Anglo-French Declaration to which reference has already been made.

It is not really easy to see how, in view of these promises, the Balfour Declaration can be said to have been properly or justly made. It had no legal or moral validity: not legal, because the British Government had no power to make it at the time when it was made, or even subsequently, because it did not acquire any sovereignty over Palestine; not moral, because it was in contravention of the promises already made to the Arabs, who had given all the assistance required of them in pursuance of such promises and which was admitted by General Allenby to have been "invaluable". One is relieved to find, however, that the promises already made to the Arabs had not been entirely overlooked. The Declaration contained a provision–almost in the nature of a proviso–in the words, "it being clearly understood that nothing shall be done" (in the Government's endeavours to facilitate the establishment of a National Home) "which may prejudice the civil or religious rights of existing non-Jewish communities in Palestine".

This was not all. King Hussein was naturally *very* disturbed when he heard the news of this Declaration. He therefore asked for an elucidation of its meaning, and was assured by the British Government in June 1918, through what has come to be known as "Hogarth's message," that "Jewish settlement in Palestine would only be allowed in so far as would be consistent with the *political and economic freedom* of the Arab population." Read along with what was stated by the Government of the United Kingdom within three months of the issue of the Declaration, there is no room for doubt that the protection of civil rights (including political and economic freedom) of the non-Jewish population was declared to be of far greater importance, and the Jewish settlement and the establishment of a National Home were to be permitted only to the extent that they were consistent with Arab rights in Palestine.

After the First World War, the Allied Powers vested themselves with authority to draw up a code of principles known as the Covenant, which should govern the action to be taken in respect of the future administration of enemy territories, including Palestine. It was with the adoption of this code or Covenant that the League of Nations came finally into existence. The principles governing mandates, including that of

Palestine, are to be found in Article 22, paragraph 4 of which deals with the territories belonging to the Turkish Empire to the following effect:

"Certain communities formerly belonging to the Turkish Empire have reached a stage of development where their existence as independent nations can be provisionally recognized subject to the rendering of administrative advice and assistance by a Mandatory until such time as they are able to stand alone. The wishes of these communities must be a principal consideration in the selection of the Mandatory." It may also be emphasized that the principle of the well-being and development of such peoples as had ceased to be under the sovereignty of States which formerly governed them formed a sacred trust of civilization.

The Arab States contend that the Balfour Declaration was inconsistent with the provisions of the Covenant (a) because the Arabs of Palestine, whose wishes had to be of primary consideration in the selection of a mandatory, were not consulted and the choice of the mandatory was made at the San Remo Conference by the High Contracting Parties without any reference to the wishes of the communities concerned. The Arab States also contend (b) that the object of the sacred trust committed to the mandatory was to ensure the well-being and development of indigenous populations, whereas in the Mandate issued at the San Remo Conference, the claim of the Jews to reconstitute their national home in an Arab land was formally recognized. There can be, in my view, no doubt that the provisions of the Mandate issued at San Remo were in conflict with the fundamental principles of self-determination and the terms of Article 22 of the Covenant.

But, even if the Arabs of Palestine are taken to have

been duly represented by King Hussein, the Covenant of the League of Nations–to which the Hejaz as an original Member of the League of Nations was a party, and which was therefore signed on behalf of King Hussein–was not, due probably to pressure by the Arabs in Palestine, ratified by him. The King of Hejaz did not attend the San Remo Conference despite an invitation to do so; as a result, the Covenant never assumed a binding force so far as the Hejaz was concerned. That is why he was not invited to the Lausanne Conference. If the Covenant was not therefore binding on Hejaz and on the Arabs, it is not open to them, in my view, to base any argument upon it. And the other nations which had duly ratified the Covenant agreed to alter its terms, if not expressly, by necessary implication. That it was possible for the contracting parties to deviate from the terms of the original contract is not open to doubt. And if the terms of the Mandate cannot be reconciled with those of the Covenant, the latter must in my judgment give way to the former, which was not only later in point of time but appeared to have been accepted on account of British persuasion in view of the promises which they had made to the Jews.

The real difficulty, which was not realized by the Government of the United Kingdom at the time but which it came to appreciate later, lay in the fact that the terms of the Declaration were inconsistent in themselves. If the establishment in Palestine of a Jewish National Home were to be taken to imply a provision for permitting the Jews to convert themselves into a State, it would come into conflict with the other part of the Balfour Declaration which contained a clear undertaking that "nothing shall be done which may prejudice the civil and religious rights of the existing non-Jewish communities in Palestine". But even if the Declaration is not to be regarded as containing any such promise – and I am clearly of the view that it cannot be so regarded – it was bound to violate the provision as to the civil rights of non-Jewish communities, for the establishment of a National Home against their will in a part of Palestine could not but be an invasion of those rights. The fact of the matter is that, in the absence of any information as to the growth of Arab nationalism and as to the depth of Arab feelings, the creation of certain rights in a so-called "notch" of the country was agreed upon before the Allies had won the war and before the British Government could be held to have had any right to make such a Declaration. But the war had somehow to be won, and it was immaterial at the time to pause to consider the legitimacy of the means adopted to achieve that end. That is why, apparently, the rights of the people which had occupied that country and the promises of independence made to them were disregarded. But if a more charitable view of the situation may be taken, in view of what Lord Curzon is reported to have said relative to the procedure adopted in the Cabinet meeting, it is possible to conceive that Lord Balfour either knew nothing about the promises which had already been made to the Arabs or had altogether forgotten them under the pressure of the war when it was at a critical juncture, and agreed on behalf of the Government to view the establishment of a Jewish National Home in Palestine with favour. This is supported by the following speech made by Mr. Lloyd George in the Commons in June 1937:

"It was one of the darkest periods of the war when Mr. Balfour prepared his Declaration. Let me recall the circumstances to the House. At the time the French Army had mutinied, the Italian Army was on the eve of collapse, and America had hardly started preparing in earnest. There was nothing left but Britain confronting the most powerful military combination the world has ever seen. It was important for us to seek every legitimate help we could get. We came to the conclusion, from information we received from every part of the world, that it was vital we should have the sympathies of the Jewish community. I can assure the Committee that we did not come to that conclusion from any predilections or prejudices. Certainly, we had no prejudices against the Arabs, because at the moment we had hundreds and thousands of troops fighting for Arab emancipation from the Turk. In these circumstances and on the advice which we received, we decided that it was desirable to secure the sympathy and cooperation of that most remarkable community, the Jews throughout the world ..."

At all events, the words "National Home" could not have been intended to convey a Jewish State. Political rights in Palestine were not being conceded to the Jews or to the Zionists, who represented that section of Jewry which intended to colonize Palestine. Lord Balfour, in his speech of 23 March 1922 before the House of Lords, made it clear that the Zionist Organization had no attribute of political power. At that time he said:

"It is surely a very poor compliment to the British Government, to the Governor of Palestine appointed by the British Government, to the Mandates Commission under the League of Nations, whose business it is to see that the spirit as well as the letter of the Mandates is carried out, and beyond them to the Council of the League of Nations, to suppose that all these bodies will so violate every pledge that they have ever given, and every principle to which they have ever subscribed, as to use the power given them by the Peace Treaty to enable one section of the community of Palestine to oppress and dominate any other ... I cannot imagine any political interests exercised under greater safeguards than the political interests of the Arab population of Palestine. Every act of government will be jealously watched. The Zionist Organization has no attribution of political powers. If it uses or usurps political powers, it is an act of usurpation. Whatever else may happen in Palestine, of this I am very confident, that under British government no form of tyranny, racial or religious, will be permitted."

It may be said that this speech referred to the Zionist Organization and not to the Jews or any other Jewish agency. But this criticism would be incorrect, for there were only two groups of thought at the time–those who wanted to have a national home in Palestine and those who did not. The Zionist Organization held one view, and there was no other society or organization which was asking for any power in Palestine besides the Zionists. That is why Lord Balfour referred to the Zionist Organization.

Nor had the Zionists themselves ever suggested the establishment of a Jewish State in Palestine until recently. This is borne out by a letter written by Dr. Theodore Herzl, the father of the Zionist movement, to M. Youssuf Zia Al-Khalidi in 1899 [*see* Appendix]. Although the former did not succeed in persuading the Sultan of Turkey to grant him permission to colonize Palestine with Jews, for which permission he was prepared to pay a large sum of money, it is abundantly clear that the idea of having any political rights in Palestine had not then occurred, or that, in any case, it was nowhere suggested. Even Dr. Weizmann, in an interview in *The Times* on 1 March 1918, had said:

"We do not aspire to found a Zionist State. What we want is a country in which all nations and all creeds shall have equal rights and equal tolerance."

This was put to him when he appeared before the Special Committee, and although he did not remember if he had made that statement, he stated that a public man's speeches might not be quoted to him after twenty-five years when a great many changes had taken place in the meantime. But in trying to interpret the Balfour Declaration, the statements made by those who were either parties or privy to its making, either at the time when it was made or shortly thereafter, and long before any desire to form a Jewish State was expressed, are not only relevant but, in my opinion, important.

Mr. Leonard Stein, a Zionist of repute, considered the idea of the return of Jews to Palestine to be more in the nature of a spiritual return. He wrote to the following effect:

"The Palestine of which they dream had for most of them long ceased to be the Palestine of concrete reality. Of its geographical position or of its physical form they knew little or nothing. They were not bound to it by ties of personal affection, nor haunted by memories of its sights and sounds. It was not indeed a mere abstraction. The return of the exiles assuredly would be a return in the most literal sense. But it would not come as the result of human effort. It would come in God's good time with the appearance of the Messiah."

Bearing the later achievements of the Zionists in mind, it is possible to argue that they had intended to claim political power and rights in Palestine from the beginning and that in order to avoid a refusal and opposition by the Arabs or even by the British Government, at the time, it was not considered discreet to ask for those rights expressly. This might or might not have been so; but the formula evolved in the modest words "National Home" was, although *ex facie* innocent, ambiguous and capable of being pressed into service (as is now being done) to secure political rights. But to an ordinary reader, it merely conveyed a "home" in the cultural sense and in no other, and the Jews would have been content with it if the subsequent developments had not been as encouraging as they turned out to be.

From what I have said, it would seem to follow that the words "National Home" in the Balfour Declaration were not intended to convey a Jewish State. Indeed, Mr. Norman Bentwich, a Jewish international lawyer of repute, defined "Jewish National Home" in or about 1926 in his book, *The Mandates System,* as a "territory in which a people *without receiving rights of political sovereignty* has nevertheless a recognized legal position and the hope of developing its moral, social and intellectual ideas". Had the idea of a possible Jewish State promised to them by the Balfour Declaration come to be known to the Jews, Mr. Bentwich could not have defined the "National Home" in that manner.

There is nothing in the Balfour Declaration, moreover, which would indicate what the Zionist aspirations were with which His Britannic Majesty's Government was declaring itself in sympathy. Nor is there anything therein to suggest that the Government of the United Kingdom had agreed to lend its hand in the establishment of a National Home. The words, "will use their best endeavours to facilitate the achievement of this object" were in keeping with the rest of the Declaration in their vagueness.

No difficulty would have been created if the matter had rested there. But in furtherance of the promise made by the Government of the United Kingdom, the Mandate for Palestine was assigned to it, apparently at its own suggestion, by the Supreme Council of the Allied Powers at San Remo in 1920; and the assignment was subsequently approved by the Council of the League of Nations in 1922. It is surprising to find, however, that the principle of self-determination contained in the Covenant of the League of Nations was absolutely disregarded, and the Mandate was approved without consulting the Arabs and in spite of their protests. It is true that President Wilson had, probably in view of the resolutions passed at the General Syrian Congress in Damascus (which combined demands for the recognition of the independence of Syria, including Palestine, as a sovereign State with repudiation of the Balfour Declaration), appointed a commission (known as the King-Crane Commission) on the mandates for former Turkish territory. But this Commission's report, which is of considerable importance in so far as it had analysed the Zionist movement quite carefully and arrived at the conclusion that the consummation of the Zionist desire for a complete dispossession of the non-Jewish inhabitants of Palestine (mark the absence of a declaration that they wanted to turn it into a Jewish State) would be, even if achieved, "a gross violation of the rights of the principle just quoted" (contained in President Wilson's address of 4 July 1918) "and of the people's rights". The King-Crane Commission recommended "that only a greatly reduced Zionist programme be attempted by the Peace Conference and even that only very gradually initiated. This would have to mean that Jewish immigration should be definitely limited and that the project for making Palestine distinctly a Jewish commonwealth should be given up." This report warned that the anti-Zionist feeling in Palestine and Syria "is intense and not lightly to be flouted." It was also reported that "from the point of view of the desires of the 'people concerned' the

Mandate should clearly go to America". The following passage from the report is, in view of what has happened, deserving of special notice:

"The people repeatedly showed honest fear that in British hands the mandatory Power would become simply a colonizing Power of the old kind; that Great Britain would find it difficult to give up the colonial theory, especially in case of a people thought inferior; that she would favour a civil service and pension budget too expensive for a poor people; that the interests of Syria *(Taken here to include Palestine)* would be subordinated to the supposed needs of the Empire; that there would be, after all, too much exploitation of the country for Britain's benefit, that she would never be ready to withdraw and give the country real independence; that she did not really believe in universal education, and would not provide adequately for it; and that she already had more territory in her possession–in spite of her fine colonial record–than was good either for herself or for the world."

No attention was paid to the King-Crane Commission's report, and the Mandate for Palestine was assigned to Great Britain. The principal obligations of the mandatory Power as defined in article 2 of the Mandate were:

(a) The creation of conditions which would secure the establishment of the Jewish National Home;
(b) The creation of conditions which would secure the development of self-governing institutions;
(c) The safeguarding of the civil and religious rights of all the inhabitants.

Article 2 of the Mandate, however, refers to the preamble which contains the statement that the Balfour

Declaration had recognized "the historical connection of the Jewish people with Palestine" and "the grounds for reconstituting their national home in that country". Actually, there is nothing in the Balfour Declaration to that effect.

It has been suggested by the Jewish Agency that the primary purpose of the Mandate was the establishment of a national home for the Jews, and that the protection of the rights and well-being of the non-Jewish population was of only secondary importance and could be kept in view only to the extent that it was compatible with the Mandate's primary purpose. This is incorrect. Article 2 of the Mandate mentions Article 22 of the Covenant of the League of Nations and refers specifically to the terms contained in the Balfour Declaration. I have already tried to show that the "civil and religious right of the existing non-Jewish population" were, although referred to later in the Declaration, not meant to be subordinated to the intention of establishing in Palestine a national home for the Jews. In fact, according to my reading, the reference towards the end of the Declaration, to the rights of the non-Jewish population, was meant for emphasis, with the object of imposing a condition on the establishment of a national home. Article 2 of the Mandate brings this out fairly clearly and leaves no room for doubt when it is read with article 6 of the same instrument, Article 6 imposes an obligation on the Administration of Palestine in the words, "while ensuring that the rights and position of other sections of the population are not prejudiced" it "shall facilitate Jewish immigration under suitable conditions".

The Mandate, as already stated, was brought into force on 29 September 1928, although the mandatory Power had in fact assumed the civil administration under the

High Commissioner from 1 July 1920, i.e., shortly after the Mandate for Palestine was assigned to the United Kingdom by the Supreme Council of the Allied Powers at San Remo. With the assumption of administration, the representative of the mandatory Power had, in furtherance of the promise contained in the Balfour Declaration, allowed Jews from all parts of the world–mostly those brought up in the Western culture and mode of living–to immigrate into Palestine, a country in the Middle East which had an Asiatic culture and was the cradle of the three greatest religions of the world.

No attention appears to have been paid by the Government of the United Kingdom, by the nations which were signatories to the Mandate, or by the representatives of the mandatory Power in Palestine to what this conglomeration of different cultures and ideals would lead to. The result of this omission can be seen by any person who visits not only Tel Aviv, Mount Carmel in Haifa, and other places, but even Jerusalem (Al-Quds) itself. Whatever may be said in favour of the development of these various towns in Palestine on Western lines, the Western mode of living may not be regarded as an unmixed blessing; it has brought a number of things in its wake which may not be very desirable, and are certainly out of place in a Holy Land.

...

The real point, however, is that the Jews from various other parts of the world had nothing in common with the Jews in Palestine except their religion; and the followers of a faith cannot be found to have any political rights in a country simply because they believe or profess to believe in that faith. Most of the Jews brought from the central portions of Europe were Aryans–descendants of people who had accepted Judaism as their faith–and it would be a travesty of facts, however much it may be utilized for the purpose of propaganda for the creation of a Jewish State, to label the dislike for the Zionists as one based on anti-Semitic feelings. The Jews were allowed to live peacefully in the Arab world without being harassed, and it was only when some of them started clamouring for political power and turned themselves into an aggressive Zionist group for the purpose of converting Palestine or a portion of it into a Jewish State that all the trouble started. It might be mentioned here that there are considerable numbers of Jews in Palestine, in America and elsewhere who do not want a Jewish State. The memorandum of the Hebrew fraction of the Jewish population in the Holy Land, dated 17 July 1947, and the memorandum of the American Council for Judaism may *inter* alia be referred to with advantage in this connexion.

The underlying causes of the disturbances of 1930, as of previous riots, were found by the Royal Commission in its report to be:
(i) The desire of the Arabs for national independence;
(ii) Their hatred and fear of the establishment of the Jewish National Home.

The following comments on these two causes were made by the Royal Commission:

"We make the following comments on these two causes:
"(i) They were the same underlying causes as those which brought about the 'disturbances' of 1920, 1921, 1929 and 1933.
"(ii) They were, and always have been, inextricably linked together. The Balfour Declaration and the Mandate under which it was to be implemented involved the denial of national independence at the

outset. The subsequent growth of the National Home created a practical obstacle, and the only serious one, to the concession later of national independence. It was believed that its further growth might mean the political as well as economic subjection of the Arabs to the Jews, so that, if ultimately the Mandate should terminate and Palestine become independent, it would not be national independence in the Arab sense but self-government by a Jewish majority."

I agree with the diagnosis and would like to add that, in my view, the unanimous attitude of the Arab States is largely, if not solely, due to similar apprehensions entertained by them; for these States appear to be fully convinced in their minds that the creation of even a small Jewish State in a part of Palestine is, with the Jewish influence, means and urge for a State, merely the thin end of the wedge and would end in disturbing the peace not only of the Middle East but probably of other parts of the world as well. One has only to compare the modest demand of 1917 for a "National Home" with the demands for a State coupled with the continuous terrorist and other military activities of the Haganah, the Irgun and the Stern Gang in support of the apprehensions. I feel that a grave error of judgment was committed, although with the best of intentions, when the Jewish Agency was allowed not merely to collaborate with the Administration of the country, but was permitted to run its own educational, industrial and economic system for a portion of the population, and thus to run a parallel government. In a place like Palestine, with the High Commissioner as the representative of the mandatory Power and in the absence of any definite plan for the self-government of the country as a whole, the whole of this Administration should have been centralized in him and he should have been asked to control the whole policy.

According to The Political History of Palestine under British Administration, presented on the latter's behalf, 99,806 Jewish immigrants were brought into the country between September 1920 and the end of 1929. Referring to this increased immigration, the Anglo-American Committee of Inquiry observed the following:

"The population, which in 1922 stood at 757,000 persons, of whom more than eleven per cent were Jews, increased by 1929 to 960,000, of whom more than sixteen per cent were Jews. This increase in the Jewish percentage appeared highly alarming to the Arab leaders.

"In 1929 Arab dissatisfaction with the Mandate and the modified Jewish National Home of the White Paper showed itself in serious riots. A new statement of policy appeared necessary to the Shaw Commission which investigated the disturbances, and in October 1930, the Passfield White Paper was issued." ...

The White Paper appeased the Arabs to some extent and the revolt came to an end. But inasmuch as the terms of this paper, on account of Jewish agitation, were materially changed by an authoritative interpretation placed upon it by the then Prime Minister, Mr. Ramsay MacDonald, the Arabs again became dissatisfied and, finding that the Jewish population had risen from over 11 per cent in 1922 to nearly 30 per cent, serious riots, which were regarded as rebellion because of their intensity, eventually broke out again in April 1936. A Royal Commission was accordingly appointed on 7 August 1936, with Earl Peel as its Chairman, to carry out the following tasks:

"To ascertain the underlying causes of the disturbances which broke out in Palestine in the middle of April; to inquire into the manner in which the Mandate for Palestine is being implemented in relation to our obligations as mandatory towards the Arabs and the Jews respectively; and to ascertain whether, upon a proper construction of the terms of the Mandate, either the Arabs or the Jews have any legitimate grievances on account of the way in which the Mandate has been, or is being implemented; and if the Commission is satisfied that any such grievances are well founded, to make recommendations for their removal and for the prevention of their recurrence."

The report of this Commission, to which I have already referred in passing for its statement of the underlying causes of the disturbances, was very carefully written. The whole situation was stated, if I may say so with respect, with considerable dexterity and circumspection, and one can find very little in its factual statements with which one can differ. Its conclusions are summarized in paragraphs 85-88 (pages 21-23) of The Political History of Palestine under British Administration and need not be recapitulated.

I must say, however, with great deference, that its final recommendation for partition of Palestine, made with the object of removing grievances and preventing their recurrence, could not have been accepted. It did not redress the Arab grievances, and regarded some form of a via media to be the best form of a solution. A technical commission (the Woodhead Commission) was appointed by the Government of the United Kingdom to examine the details of a partition scheme, in accordance with the League Council's resolution.

The members of the Woodhead Commission were not agreed amongst themselves, although they were unanimous in rejecting the proposal made by the Royal Commission. One of them was of the view that no practicable scheme of partition could be devised, while the majority recommended "a plan which would have confined the Jewish State to a strip of territory approximately 75 kilometres in length but intersected by an Arab enclave at Jaffa and the corridor connecting the mandated territory of Jerusalem with the sea". The report was considered by the Government of the United Kingdom, which rejected the suggested solution on the ground of impracticability (Command 5893).

An attempt was then made by the British Government to reach an agreement in consultation with the Arabs and the Jews. A conference was accordingly called, but met with no success. Another White Paper was then issued by the British Government on 17 May 1939. (A summary of this Paper is given in paragraphs 102-108, pages 27-29 of The Political History of Palestine under British Administration.) It was unequivocally declared by His Britannic Majesty's Government that it was "not part of their Policy that Palestine should become a Jewish State" and that the objective was "the establishment within ten years of an independent Palestine State . . , in which Arabs and Jews share in government in such a way as to ensure that the essential interests of each community are safeguarded." The Government was of the view that "to seek to expand the National Home indefinitely by immigration against the strongly expressed will of the Arab people of the country" would not only be contrary to the whole spirit of Article 22 of the League Covenant, but also to its specific obligations to the Arabs in the Palestine Mandate itself. Taking into consideration, therefore, "the extent to which the growth of the Jewish National

Home has been facilitated over the last twenty years", the Government came to the decision that it could be further expanded only if the Arabs were prepared to acquiesce in this growth. It was therefore ordered that, after the admission of not more than 75,000 additional immigrants during the five years beginning in April 1939, the immigration would be stopped unless the Arabs of Palestine were prepared to agree to further immigration.

The policy expounded in the White Paper was bitterly criticized by the Jews but it was accepted by the British Parliament. It came up for consideration by the Permanent Mandates Commission at its 86th Session in June 1939. The Commission was unanimously of the view that "the policy set out in the White Paper was not in accordance with the interpretation" which it had so far been putting upon the Mandate, along with the mandatory Power; but there was divergence of opinion on the points whether the policy was in harmony with the Mandate and whether it could be justified in the existing circumstances if it were not opposed by the Council of the League of Nations.

The White Paper of 1939 is an extremely important document, not only because it contains a definition of British policy after all that had been happening in Palestine since 1920 but also because it contains the authorized and well considered interpretation of the Balfour Declaration. The policy set out in the White Paper might not have been in accordance with the interpretation placed upon the Mandate up to that time by the Permanent Mandates Commission or by the mandatory Power. But the latter could not possibly ignore the circumstances under which it had operated or the situation which its operation had produced in the country. The number of Jews in Palestine had increased to about ten times what it had been when the administration was taken over by Great Britain and when the so-called National Home, which could in no use be unlimited in its development, was rightly regarded to have come into being in accordance with the promises contained in the Declaration and the Mandate. This statement might not have been found suitable to the Jews, but the charge that it was in any way opposed to the previous declarations of the British Government is groundless.

Moreover, the policy of permitting unlimited immigration was nowhere suggested in the Mandate, which purported to give effect to Article 22 of the League of Nations Covenant and to the provisions of the Balfour Declaration, which contained the clause that nothing should be done which would prejudice the civil and religious rights of existing non-Jewish communities in Palestine. The result was that the Covenant could not be held to have been superseded or modified in this respect by any international instrument.

It might be added that, in pursuance of what was contained in the Mandate, the mandatory Power had, besides permitting a very large amount of immigration, allowed the Jewish enterprise of rapid economic expansion to grow by granting concessions of great value to the Palestine Potash Co., Ltd. in the Dead Sea, and to the Palestine Electric Corporation. The number of Jewish agricultural settlements had, according to page 15 of The Political History of Palestine under British Administration risen from 96 in 1927 to 172 in 1936; the volume of citrus exports had gone up from 2,600,000 cases in 1929 to 15,300,000 in 1938-1939.

Considering all that had happened in Palestine, there can be no manner of doubt that the National Home, unless it was taken to mean a Jewish State with a Jewish majority, had come into being and that the mandatory Power was fully justified in coming to a decision that things should not be allowed to continue to drift as they had been allowed to do.

Following the declaration of the policy in the White Paper of 1939, acts of terrorism began to be committed by the Jews, who also attempted to organize the unauthorized entry of a large number of immigrants. But the Second World War started early in September 1939 and both Jews and Arabs were requested by their respective leaders to render full assistance to the Government of the United Kingdom. The attention of the Jews and Arabs was to some extent directed into other channels, but unauthorized immigration and some terrorist activities by the Jews continued to a limited extent even in this period. With the termination of the war, however, the Jews began to intensify their efforts toward unauthorized immigration, and a series of outrages of varying intensity began to be committed. These still continue in almost unabated vigour. Despite all this, immigration was allowed by the Government of Palestine to continue at the rate of 15,000 a year although the five years referred to in the White Paper of 1939 had long since expired and the quota of 75,000 which it permitted during the five years had been exhausted.

Thanks to Germany's anti-Semitic attitude and its cruel, callous and inhuman massacres of Jewry during the last world war, the Zionists, who by no means formed a majority of the Jews before the war, began to clamour more vociferously for political rights in Palestine. They succeeded in securing a good many supporters from amongst those who were not in the beginning prepared to support their co-religionists in their attempt to form themselves into a political State. This fact, however, led the Arabs, both Christians and Moslems, to unite and to resist this attempt with all the means at their command.

Thus, the renaissance movement which had started amongst the Arabs toward the middle of the last century came to be strengthened to a large extent. The pressure exerted by Zionism on the mandatory Power and on the United States of America by well-organized propaganda led the British Government to ask the United Nations to consider the problem presented by Palestine: a small, uneven and rocky country rightly described to be no bigger than Wales, and covered by fairly large areas here and there which are uncultivated, and some of which have been and are perhaps uncultivable, but which are nevertheless equally, if not more, holy to Christians and Moslems as well.

Since the demand in the United States was strong, President Truman suggested to the Prime Minister of Britain that 100,000 immigration certificates should be issued, but since the latter could not adopt the proposal before the future of Palestine had been fully reconsidered in the light of all that had happened, the Governments of both agreed to appoint an Anglo-American Committee of Inquiry. This Committee rejected partition as a solution of the problem created by Palestine, and held that the establishment of an independent State or States in Palestine would result in civil strife which might threaten the peace of the world. Thus, we find that the land which has sent the messages of peace and good will to the world on a number of occasions is asking for peace itself. But since it could not find a solution, the Anglo-American Committee of Inquiry recommended that Palestine should continue to be administered under the Mandate pending the execution of a trusteeship agreement.

There is no denying the fact, however, that the attitude of the British Government, however justified by the exigency of the situation as it presented itself to that Government in 1914, has led to the present impasse which is largely of its creation. Speaking for myself, I consider the British Government, rather than any other Power, to be primarily responsible for the situation in which the United Nations find themselves now placed. It had not only agreed to facilitate the establishment of a Jewish National Home in Palestine after its promises of independence to the Arabs, which were reiterated in 1918 and later, but in its intense desire to keep control of the Middle East and to keep France out, it secured the Mandate assignment from the Supreme Council of the Allied Powers at San Remo in 1920 and got the assignment approved by the Council of the League of Nations in July 1922.

In anticipation of this approval, the British Government had Palestine under its control in 1920, and started its endeavours to facilitate the establishment of the National Home in all earnest almost immediately, so much so that no less than 5,514 Jews were allowed to immigrate between September and December 1920, despite various Arab protests and riots which had started almost immediately. It continued to pursue this policy with great vigour between 1920 and 1925, and succeeded in bringing 89,666 persons into Palestine between 1920 and 1926. As the number of immigrants was increasing every year, the Arabs' fears of losing their country were increasing and Arab protests and riots were proportionately growing in intensity. These were being curbed relentlessly but could not be suppressed until 1939, when the White Paper was finally issued and, in fact, when the Second World War began in September of that year.

During this period, hundreds of Arabs were killed, thousands were put into prison, and a number of houses were destroyed. There was a reign of terror, and the Jews, who now naturally resent the use of security measures, were themselves eager for the legislation which is now being used against them. During such a disturbed state of affairs, it was impossible for the Arabs to develop their land and take part in the peaceful pursuits which go to develop a nation. In the meantime, however, the Jews who were siding with the Government lost no time in trying to consolidate their position. With the help of large sums of money which they were getting from the Jewry of the world, particularly those of America, industries were being developed and lands were being acquired from the Arabs. Many of the latter, not being rich, were, as a result of the constant friction between themselves and the Government, reduced to penury. I can only visualize what, in such circumstances, their plight must have been. It is therefore not surprising to find that the Jews succeeded in securing large plots of land at the moderate prices prevailing at the time. At the same time, it might be mentioned that the only bank which was advancing money to agriculturists (the Ottoman Agriculturist Bank) was liquidated in 1922. Being engaged in what they regarded as a fight for independence, the Arabs' condition must have been, financially speaking, pitiable. These two decades of unrest were bound to affect seriously their advancement and development in almost every walk of life. That they were able to survive against two formidable opponents speaks volumes for their energy and determination.

The Administration of the mandatory Power does not seem to have done much during the last twenty-seven years in the way of uplifting the indigenous people of the country, a task which, as an agent of the mandatory Power, it was obliged to do. To say nothing of secondary and higher education, even elementary education was ignored; and despite the fact that nearly three decades have elapsed, the number of schools in the country is not large enough and admittedly thousands of Arab boys desirous of receiving education are disappointed every year. There are no vocational institutions, and those who wish to receive vocational education must either go to the American University in Beirut or to foreign countries for this purpose.

Nothing appears to have been done during this time to train persons for social service. While millions of pounds have been and are being spent on security measures and on the armed police, which is a more or less permanent fixture of the country, sufficient attention has not been paid to opening hospitals and health centres. One of the most serious defects of Ottoman administration, the system of land tenancy, has not been sufficiently altered to develop initiative in the fellaheen. No serious attempts seem to have been made to introduce measures which would have led to self-government. The two half-hearted attempts made at considerable intervals were not enough. These were really due to the conflict with the Arabs during the first years of the Administration, and with the Jews during the last eight years. The fact remains, however, that the mandatory Power cannot be held to have succeeded in preparing the people for self-government, and the purpose for which the Mandate was granted under Article 22 of the Covenant must be found not to have been achieved.

Moreover, the international machinery in the form of the Permanent Mandates Commission, which had been created for the purpose of scrutinizing the actions of the mandatory Powers, and to which they were bound to submit annual reports, has, along with the League of Nations, ceased to exist. There are no means by which the international obligations in regard to mandates can be discharged by the United Nations.

The Mandate has in any case become infructuous, and must, in my opinion, go. Whether it could be superseded by any other system within the present Charter is a different matter, and will be dealt with when I consider the solution of the present problem.

But what the mandatory has done in allowing the immigration of hundreds of thousands of persons ever since the Mandate has been in force cannot be undone. Private rights have been created. People have been allowed to come and settle down. They cannot be asked to go. The objection that most of them have not acquired Palestinian citizenship and owe double loyalties at the present moment has considerable force. But those who have been allowed to spend time and labour by a Power discharging what it considered to be its duty under an international instrument cannot be lightly treated, although to impose conditions which would enable these people to acquire Palestinian citizenship within a reasonable time would be just and proper. If they do not take advantage of the time which may be granted to them, and do not make up their minds finally to become Palestinian citizens, they will have to remain in the country as foreigners. But if they do, they will have all the rights which the indigenous population possesses in its own country.

For the above reasons, I am of the opinion that the questions formulated in the beginning should be answered as follows:

(a) That the Balfour Declaration should not have been made;

(b) That the Mandate was in conflict with, and inconsistent with, the Covenant of the League of Nations;

(c) That the Mandate was in the circumstances to prevail in preference to the Covenant when and where it was found to be inconsistent with the latter;

(d) That the legal effect of the Mandate is that the actions taken by the mandatory Power in discharge of its obligations, or what it regarded to be its obligations, are valid and that the immigrants who have been allowed to come into Palestine cannot be turned out, although under the rules now in force they must be required to acquire Palestinian citizenship within a reasonable time if they wish to have the rights of citizens in that country. But nations had no right to create a Mandate over Palestine without the consent of its inhabitants and to impose their will upon them.

Although, strictly speaking, the Mandate cannot be held to have conferred any rights over Palestine *de jure,* it must be found to have acquired a *de facto* validity as it has been enforced. But with the declaration of the mandatory Power that it has found the Mandate to be unworkable, with the abolition of the Permanent Mandates Commission which could scrutinize the mandatory Powers' actions, and with the fact that the promise of the Jewish National Home has been, as conceded by the mandatory Power, fulfilled, the Mandate ceases to have further effect. That is why I would recommend its termination.

(III) PROPOSAL FOR FORM OF GOVERNMENT

This brings us to the most important question–that of the future form of government which Palestine should have. Before dealing with this question, however, it appears to me necessary to review briefly the respective contentions advanced by the Jews and the Arabs.

The Jewish claim to have the whole of Palestine as a Jewish State, or to have a Jewish State in a fairly large portion of Palestine, has been based on:
(a) The historical association of the Jews with Palestine;
(b) The religious significance which they attach to Palestine;
(c) The improvements effected by them at considerable cost, and the resulting increase in Palestine's economic prosperity;
(d) Their "homelessness";
(e) The promises contained in the Balfour Declaration, subsequently incorporated in the Mandate, and agreed to by a large number of nations;
(f) Jewish persecution generally throughout the world, and particularly the massacres by Hitler during the Second World War.

The Jews came to be associated with Palestine, or "Eretz Israel", historically when the tribe of Abraham, originating in Ur of the Chaldees in the Euphrates Valley, settled in a portion of Palestine about 1400 B.C. It is true that Abraham's descendants, David and Solomon, had small kingdoms in a part of Palestine. But these came to an end with the latter's death and after a chequered history, during long periods of which all the inhabitants of Palestine (including Jews) remained under subjection to the Assyrians, the Babylonians and the Romans. The Jews were expelled from the land at the beginning of the Christian era. To found their claim on their dispersion from Palestine after a period of approximately 2,000 years, whatever religious sentiment may be attached by them to the land occupied by their Prophets, appears to me to be as groundless as anything can be.

A multitude of nations conquered various countries at various times and were eventually defeated and turned out of them. Can their connexion, however long, with the land which they had once conquered provide them with any basis after the lapse of even one century?

If this were so, Moslems might claim Spain, which they governed for a much longer period than the Jews had governed part of Palestine. The religious attachment can form no foundation for such a claim, for religious sentiment is one thing and political rights another. Can the Moslems scattered throughout the world who turn their faces to the Caaba five times a day when they say their prayers claim any political rights in Mecca, which is now under the sovereignty of His Majesty King Ibn Saud?

This is not all. We are apt to become confused if we do not analyse the fact that, whatever claim may be advanced to justify the return of Jews to the land from which their ancestors had been dispossessed, this claim cannot be made by those who were subsequently converted to Judaism. Khazars of Eastern Europe, Turco Finn by race, were converted to Judaism as a nation about 690 A.D. Can their descendants possibly claim any rights simply because the ancestors of their co-religionists had once settled in Palestine?

It is absolutely wrong to suggest that the profession of a faith by a person–and that is all that Mr. Shertok suggested in his statement–clothes him with any political rights in a country. In fact, most of the blue-eyed and blond Jews that I happened to see in Jerusalem appeared to be as much Aryans as any German. Most of the Jews from Central Europe or the Baltic countries have striking resemblance to the Aryans of those countries. Can brown-skinned Jews in Abyssinia and yellow-skinned Jews in China be regarded to be of the same race? It should not be forgotten that there was considerable missionary activity in ancient and medieval times and that it led to mass conversions. An extract from an article in the *Encyclopedia Britannica* by a well-known Jewish scholar who was at one time Professor of Hebrew at Oxford University, Dr. H. M. J. Loewe, refers to the proselytizing effort made by the Jews in converting pagans. He writes:

"The Jew, when confronted with paganism, omnipotent and universal, has engaged in active proselytization ... and classical authors testify to the vigour of the Jewish missionary enterprise."

In his book, *Race and Civilization (Pages 132-133)*, Frederick Hertz wrote in 1927 that:

"Conversions to the Jewish religion of Greeks, Romans and other nationalities occurred very frequently, especially during the last two centuries B.C.; and in the Middle Ages and modern times, notwithstanding all obstacles, such conversions have happened occasionally, chiefly in the Slav countries, this being evidently the reason why the Polish and Russian Jews frequently have unmistakable Slav facial characteristics."

It is unnecessary to develop the point any further. The contention advanced on behalf of the Jews can have no bearing on Jews whose ancestors were not turned out of Palestine, and has no force, even in the case of those who have descended from such ancestors, inasmuch as after a lapse of centuries they cannot possibly have any claim to political rights in a land which they left some 2,000 years ago.

I have already dealt with the question of religious significance, and it appears to be unnecessary to say very much more. I would, however, like to add that the Prophets of the Jews are regarded as Prophets both by Christians and Moslems. Moslems regard Christ as a Prophet and place him in the same category in which the Jews place their own Prophets. Thus, the land which is holy to the Jews because of Abraham, Moses, Isaac, etc. is equally holy to Christians and Moslems; and the land in which Christ was born and lived is also holy to Moslems, although the Jews do not regard Christ as a Prophet.

The fact that the Jews of the world were permitted to immigrate in and after 1920 and spent considerable sums of money in improving a part of Palestine cannot confer any political rights upon them. If this argument were to be upheld, it would amount to saying that, by spending any amount of money in the improvement of a house or land, the person who has spent the money gets title to the same–a very dangerous and wholly unsound proposition. But whatever the value of the argument, it cannot possibly have any force when we find that the money was being spent in spite of the Arabs' protests to increase Jewish immigration and to consolidate the Jews' position. These improvements *have* perhaps indirectly benefited the Arabs, but this does not advance the argument, for it must be remembered that all the efforts appear to have been directed towards improving Palestine with the object of converting it into a Jewish State. The gain of *some* temporary advantages or benefit to the Arabs cannot be regarded as any compensation for the loss of the country as a whole.

The contention that the Jews need a State because they are homeless and have no other State which they can call their own does not bear close examination. Can they for the same reason ask for New York State, which has well over three million Jews already, or for England? But the United States of America and England are strong enough to resist a demand by force of arms if necessary. Or is it Palestine, where immigration has been carried out to a large extent with the help of the mandatory Power's forces, because it is considered unable to defend itself against the forces which the Jews have organized? I fear that the Jews, who are not and cannot be regarded to be either a nation or a race, have on account of an urge for a State, big or small, resolved to have Palestine or a portion of the same as a Jewish State. The Jews are in the minority even today. But they want to have the help of the United Nations (help which the mandatory Power has refused to give them in accordance with the principle enunciated by it in the White Paper of 1939) to permit them through immigration to become a majority first, and then to ask for the principle of self determination to be applied to them.

The whole of this effort is as unreasonable as anything can be. If we are called upon to adjudicate on the question of the future government, we have to take the facts as they exist today and decide on the material before us. It is wrong, in my view, to wait for events which may or may not happen in the future and decide our course on the assumption that they have already come to pass. The whole argument advanced by the Jews is based on unrealities, and the fact that they are homeless and desire to have a State cannot possibly be taken into consideration as conferring any right upon them to have it.

I have already dealt with the Balfour Declaration separately. The Mandate, whatever its validity, has succeeded in establishing a National Home.

It is unfortunately true that the Jews were persecuted by Hitler during the Second World War, but whatever sympathy one may have for his victims, the problem of displaced persons is not only a question of entry into Palestine, as the Jews would have us hold, but a question for the whole world to settle. Fortunately or unfortunately, the world is divided into a number of national States; it is their right to regulate immigration within their own boundaries and to determine the composition of their population. If Palestine is to have the same independence enjoyed by the other countries of the world, the same right should be conceded to the future Government of an independent Palestine. Immigration into Palestine would have to be controlled by the Palestinian Government with due regard to the interests and welfare of the existing population. Palestine would have to bear its share of displaced persons in the future; but in deciding that question, the number of immigrants, both legal and illegal, who have already entered the country should be taken into account.

The Arabs' case, on the other hand, is essentially that they are the descendants of indigenous inhabitants who were in the country even before Abraham settled in it; that even after the Islamic conquest in the seventh century, the conquerors, (who had succeeded in giving their language, their culture and their religion to the people of Palestine) were themselves assimilated into the existing population which, along with its descendants, remained in continuous possession of the country. It is conceded that the Turks conquered the country in the middle of the sixteenth century, but it is contended that despite this conquest the indigenous inhabitants of the country continued to take part in the government, and although nominally the sovereignty rested in the Turkish Empire, they were an integral part of that Empire and took part in its government. Finally, it is urged that at all events the Arabs constituted and still constitute a large majority of the inhabitants of Palestine.

According to the well-known international principle of self-determination, which is now universally recognized and forms a keystone of the Charter of the United Nations, the affairs of a country must be conducted in accordance with the wishes of the majority of its inhabitants. In 1947, it is too late to look at the matter from any other angle. And thus looked at, the claim put forward by the Arabs is unanswerable and must be conceded, although it would be highly undesirable–nay, almost impossible–to overlook important minorities, such as the Jews in Palestine happen to be at present.

It is true that the political sovereignty of Palestine under Ottoman rule was vested in the Sultan of Turkey. But it must be remembered that the Arabs were not satisfied with their political status in spite of the rights which they enjoyed under that regime, and the Arab renaissance movement started about the middle of the last century. This was not liked by the Turks, and steps were taken by them to curb the movement. Several secret societies which came into being thirty or forty years later gave great impetus to the movement. The

Turkish Empire was gradually disintegrating, and the Committee of Union and Progress, composed as it was of Young Turks, although successful in forcing Sultan Abdul Hamid to abdicate, found it difficult to control the Arab drive for independence. And when Turkey joined Germany in the First World War, the Arabs lost no opportunity to achieve that object and, through King Hussein, negotiated with the British Government for their freedom.

Turkey was defeated in 1918, and the Arabs felt that their dream of independence would then be realized. But the British Government had, in the meantime, issued the Balfour Declaration. On receipt of this news, while the war was still in progress, Arab suspicion was aroused; and on a question put by King Hussein the Arabs' doubts were allayed, as already mentioned, by the "Hogarth message." In it the Arabs were assured that the establishment of the Jewish National Home would be *subject to the political and economic freedom of the Arabs.*

In any case, they were in the majority and continue to be so, despite the large immigration of Jews into the country during the last twenty seven years. The Arabs are, as admitted by the Rt. Hon. Mr. Bevin, no less advanced than the people of the other Arab countries, which have already secured their independence. Thus, there is no reason whatsoever why they should not be allowed to manage their own country and form their own government. I might add, even at the risk of repetition, that Article 22, paragraph 4 of the League of Nations Covenant, which was in no way modified by the Mandate, read along with article 16 of the Treaty of Lausanne, under which the country was not renounced by the Turks in favour of the Allies, point to the same conclusion. The conclusion is thus irresistible that self-government must be granted to the people of Palestine as a whole.

I am fully aware of the persistent propaganda which has been carried on by the Jews, particularly during the last few years, with the object of getting a State for themselves. And it may be conceded that for this purpose the Zionist group has tried to produce conditions and create an atmosphere which has close resemblance to a national movement. But it is impossible to forget that the Jews, as a whole, are not a nation but only a community which follows a particular religion. The urge of the Zionists to get a State and, with that in view, to convert themselves into a nation, cannot make them a nation in spite of their riches and intelligence. A Jew in England is even today as English as Anglo-Saxons living there. Similarly, a Jew in the United States is just an American and has American nationality. Moreover, the so-called nationalism is of too recent a growth to be of any value.

The question then to consider is what form this self-government should take. The Jewish Agency demands a Jewish State in the whole of Palestine, while Dr. Weizmann in his evidence before us expressed the view that partition was the most satisfactory solution. Dr. Magnes, on the other hand, asked for a bi-national State but with parity between Arabs and Jews although the latter were not and are not numerically equal, forming about one-third of the whole population.

All three exponents of these different points of view are unanimous, however, in pressing for the free and unrestricted immigration of Jews into Palestine. That is because it is impossible for them to substantiate their claim for independence or for a State even in a part of Palestine. Evidence is not wanting that a fairly large number of Jews in Palestine are being held back by the pressure of the Jewish Agency, but nevertheless thousands of applications have been made by individual Jews to various consulates in Jerusalem for emigration. It was admitted to us by Mr. Sommerfelt of the Preparatory Commission of the International Refugee Organization that considerable propaganda is being carried on by or on behalf of the Jewish Agency in the camps for displaced persons with the object of inducing Jews to immigrate into Palestine, although he found that those staying in these camps as a general rule agree, if they are afforded opportunities, to go to places other than Palestine. The exuberance in the expression of sympathy by the Jewish Agency for those who are in displaced persons camps, and their demonstrations in trying to force illegal immigration into Palestine–of which the *Exodus 1947*, recently brought back to Port le Bouc, is a glaring instance–has a two-fold purpose, although I am not prepared to say that the feelings of sympathy for their co-religionists in trouble are entirely absent. Every human being is bound to have varying degrees of sympathy for his fellow-beings if they are in trouble, and the callous and inhuman treatment by Hitler cannot but invoke sympathy in any other human being. But I feel that these persons' misfortunes are being magnified for a political end, while we hear nothing of a much larger number of persons in these camps who are not Jews.

Looked at in the right perspective, immigration is in my judgment being insisted upon either because the Jews wish to turn the minority in Palestine into a majority or with the object of showing to the world that they were and are capable of doing so. I have my own doubts, however, whether, with the natural increase of the Arabs, they would ever be able to do so. Nor am I sure that, once the future of Palestine is settled one way or another, the Jews will give any great impetus to immigration, for if they acquire a State, they will have to look at this problem in a different manner, for obvious reasons. If they do not acquire one, then real immigration will have no political object in view. It must be remembered that these immigrants are far from being economical; they cost the Jewish Agency large sums of money to transport, maintain and establish them in Palestine. Without the huge contributions from America and elsewhere, the Agency would not have found it possible to continue this effort for any length of time.

The other possible solutions to which my attention was drawn in the meetings of the Special Committee were federation, with varying degrees of power and control at the centre, and cantonization.

The Arab States, on the other hand, pressed for the creation of a unitary State for Palestine on the basis of the present population of Arabs and of the Jews who have already acquired Palestinian citizenship. Since immigration was regarded by them in the light of an attempt by the minority to transform itself into a majority, with the help of the mandatory Power hitherto and possibly with the help of the United Nations hereafter, the Arab States strictly resisted any further immigration of Jews into Palestine and questioned the right of the British Government or even of the United Nations to impose it against the will of indigenous inhabitants, particularly since its object was to deprive the Arabs of their country either wholly or in part. The position taken by the Arab States was not purely in the interests of the Arabs of Palestine, but in their own interests as well; for the setting up of a Jewish State in their midst would be, according to them, a source of great danger to their own safety. They also apprehended that if immigration were allowed to continue, the Jews would not remain confined to the country of their occupation but would gradually begin to infiltrate into the adjoining States. This would constitute a serious menace to the peace of the Middle East.

The bi-national and cantonal solutions can be easily disposed of. The bi-national solution is opposed to the fundamental concepts of democracy, for Dr. Magnes based it on parity of Arabs and Jews in the organs of government, irrespective of their present proportions in the country's population. It is interesting to observe that in his small book, *Like All the Nations?*, published by him in 1930, Dr. Magnes observed on page 7 the following:

"A former Administrator of Palestine reckoned that, with agriculture remaining the chief industry of Palestine, the land within its present political borders could accommodate roughly 3,000,000 people. Others give higher figures. But as for myself, if I could know that in the course of a long, long period a Jewish community of 1,000,000 souls–one-third of the population–was possible here, I should be well content. There are now 900,000 people in the country, of whom 160,000 are Jews. Let the colonizers and the students of vital statistics tell us how long a period it will take for Arabs to become 2,000,000 and Jews to become 1,000,000. Surely much longer than a full generation. Why not, therefore, let us try to work out a programme for a generation, and let the generation after take care of its own problems? If we could do this, we should perhaps be talking less in abstractions, and even though we differed in our philosophies, all of us ought to be able to work together with a will."

This one-third has become one-half within a span of

seventeen years although, despite all their efforts, the Jews have succeeded in bringing up their numbers in Palestine to only one-third. A bi-national solution would also mean the setting up of a complicated system of artificial devices to attain the parity which does not exist at present and is not feasible.

The cantonal solution implies the dissection of the country into a large number of small uniform groups of Jews and Arabs, with power to govern the various *cantons*. It would actually result in creating about 200 or more local units, which would not only be cumbersome but might also lead to disorder.

If these two possibilities are ruled out, as they must be in my mind, the choice would lie between partition on the one hand, and a unitary or federal form of government on the other.

As for partition, I find that this solution, although suggested by the Royal Commission, was not accepted by the Woodhead Partition Commission which was appointed by the Government of the United Kingdom on the receipt of the Royal Commission's report. It is true that a majority of the members of the Woodhead Commission made certain proposals, but after a full consideration of all the facts these did not find favour with the Government of the United Kingdom, and were finally rejected as impracticable. The reasons given by Mr. Reed on pages 268 - 281 of the Woodhead Partition Commission Report, which did ultimately prevail, have considerable weight and I adopt them. For myself, I would like to emphasize the following reasons for the rejection of partition as affording a reasonable solution:

(a) It would not be possible to create two viable States.

(b) It would not be possible to create a Jewish State without a very large Arab minority which would be intermixed with Jews. The best of the various schemes which have been put before the Government of the United Kingdom at different times could not avoid an Arab minority of [350,000] in a Jewish State with 460,000 Jews. Such a large number of disgruntled Arabs would give rise to fresh problems similar to those which we have been called upon to consider, and would render it impossible to govern the country. Moreover, there is no reason why Arabs, who are in a majority in the whole State, should, by adopting this method, be reduced to a minority.

(c) Palestine is far too small a country to be able to bear the burden, financial and otherwise, of two governments particularly when relations between the people of the two governments are bound to be strained from the very beginning.

(d) The Jewish State would be surrounded by hostile Arab States, and there would always be a danger of war.

(e) The commerce of Palestine is already handicapped by artificial frontiers which separate it from the other Arab countries. The division of Palestine into two or more areas would create obstacles which would make impossible the transit of goods and persons.

(f) Since there is no reasonable chance of cooperation between the Arabs and Jews, the Arab boycott would probably be strengthened and the Jewish State would be forced to buy raw and other materials for its use from, and to take its products for sale to, places at long distances.

(g) If partition were carried through, the main areas where intensive cultivation is possible and the main potential centres of industry would lie within the Jewish State; and the problem of the rural population would be difficult to solve.

(h) Relations between the Arabs and the Jews are bound to deteriorate and not to improve by a partition scheme, which would have to be enforced by a special force of the United Nations. From where would the United Nations get such a force?

(i) The Arab State would consist mainly of hilly country, generally unfertile and already thickly populated by poverty-stricken people.

(j) Partition would actually do a great disservice to the Jews as a whole. Jews living elsewhere would lose the strength arising from their present nationalities and would be exposed to the embarrassing position of having a double loyalty, which would create mistrust against them in the country in which they reside. That is why a number of influential Jews like Mr. Montagu have opposed the creation of a Jewish State. For the same reason, there are a large number of Jews even now who oppose the idea.

(k) Palestine is as thickly populated now as Belgium; and if the desert portion in the south, which is mostly uncultivable, is not to be taken into account, the density of the remaining portion of the country would become worse, and be intolerable. If the Arabs' natural rate of increase is also kept in mind, partition would make Palestine an impossible country to live in. The right of self-determination has been given to the country as a whole; and a scheme of partition would, in my view, be opposed to this principle.

The confederation envisaged by some of the members of the Special Committee is no confederation at all as that term is understood in international law, but a kind of union for economic purposes only. The union proposed has all the disadvantages of a partition, yet has no advantage which a partition could have brought in its wake. It would, for instance, permit all the Jews from the Jewish State to acquire economic rights in the Arab State and thus, in fact, in the whole of Palestine. I cannot see how this union can be imposed by force. If it has to depend for its working on the consent of the two States and of the people residing therein, the only argument advanced against federation disappears. Nor can I see how it is possible to have an Arab State which is at least viable.

Foreseeing this difficulty, it has been proposed by the Committee members who favour economic union that a duty should be imposed on the Jewish State to pay a contribution from the customs earned by it to the Arab State. The payment of the amount, if it is to be in proportion to the realization, will have to depend upon the sweet will of the Jews; and the manipulation of the accounts for the purpose of making these payments is a possibility, if not a probability, which one can[not] refuse to consider. Above all, the money earned by the Jews which would have to be contributed to the Arab State would be hardly in consonance with the self-respect of the Arabs. It is well known that if the Arabs are touchy on any point, they are so on this one point more than any other.

The choice now lies between a unitary State, such as I have suggested, and a federal State. Both of these are forms of democracy. The Palestine problem has not so far been solved because attempts have been made continually to disregard the democratic principles in order to please or placate the Jews in view of their influence and riches, assisted by both an extensive and intensive propaganda carried on particularly in the United States, which has several million Jews. It is always best to stick to the right path and not to deviate from the principles which have long received international recognition. The hand of the clock cannot be set back, and we would have to enforce those principles as far as possible, deviating from the well-beaten track only if that is found to be essential in the circumstances.

It would be entirely wrong, in my opinion, for the people of Palestine to regard that country as being in some way peculiar politically, whatever importance it does possess from a religious or sentimental point of view. But there is no reason why political considerations should be mixed up with religious considerations and why political rights in a State should be confused with religious rights. Life is, I know, made up of compromises but it is not possible to compromise principles. It is impossible to minimize the importance of peace and order, and for the sake of peace and amity I am ready to accept any reasonable solution as long as I find it to be just.

Having regard to the fact that the indigenous population of the country has been in possession of the country, and agreed to throw off the yoke of the Turks during the First World War, thus throwing away whatever rights they had possessed in carrying on the government of the country at that time, I do not think it is possible to ignore the principle of self-determination and to refuse the majority the right of forming the government.

I may not, however, be understood to say that I am

willing to sacrifice the rights of the minority, whether religious, linguistic, educational or cultural rights. They must be fully protected by the constitution, which may be declared to be either absolutely unalterable or not capable of being altered unless a majority of three-fourths votes in favour of its alteration. This is, however, a matter of detail and can be settled later. The important point is that once these rights are duly protected by the constitution, there should be no legitimate reason for the Jews to apprehend that they will be ill-treated by the majority. Short of getting a separate State for themselves, with the attendant advantages and disadvantages which such a State confers, the Jews should be reasonably satisfied with the protection which I have suggested when I am ready to concede that the Jews who have already immigrated into Palestine and settled down there should be permitted to remain if they have already acquired Palestinian citizenship or will acquire it within a period of, say, two years. This is being suggested with the object of avoiding a dual loyalty to two States at one time, and at the same time to create loyalty toward the Palestinian State.

Several portions of Palestine, on account of their associations with the lawgivers of three great monotheistic religions and with their apostles and followers, have a great attraction for many millions of their adherents. There is no other land in the whole world which arouses so much religious sentiment and feeling. A focus of the spiritual interests of Jews, Christians and Moslems (of which the Wailing Wall, the Holy Sepulchre, the Mount of Olives, Haram esh-Sharif and Masjid Aqsa are only a few examples), Palestine will continue to arouse deep attachment as long as these religions continue to exist. But, as remarked by me elsewhere, religious or spiritual connexions with the land are one thing and political sovereignty another. The exercise of political sovereignty over a country has nothing to do, however, with religious rights which a sovereign may possess over the land where religious institutions or other objects of religious interest are located. The Moslems, after their conquest of Palestine in the seventh century, did not desecrate the holy places of worship. Nor have I any reason to suppose that the Palestinian State, or any person or body of persons who exercise sovereign rights in the land, would at any time interfere with the exercise of religious rights and rites in the holy buildings of individuals of the various persuasions. For the above reasons, I am convinced in my mind that there is no reason to separate Jerusalem, Bethlehem, Hebron, Galilee, etc., or to deal with them separately for political purposes. It is better, nevertheless, to guarantee the Holy Places in the constitution, which should provide:

(a) That the State would preserve the sacred character of all the Holy Places, and keep them in good repair;
(b) That, except for persons of undesirable character politically or otherwise, all pilgrims from all over the world, would be allowed access to the Holy Places in conformity with existing rights;
(c) That the State would never interfere with religious liberty and the performance of religious rites in these places.

In giving concrete shape to the conception of a free and independent Palestinian people and a Palestinian State, the leaders of the country must work for a divorce of race and religion from politics and cease to think in terms of religious persuasion when dealing with affairs of state. In so far as politics and administration are concerned, there must in the future be only a Palestinian State and a Palestinian people. To such a laical and such a people we must give the independence which any other country in the world enjoys. The idea of a separate Jewish nation and a separate Arab nation within Palestine should not be countenanced.

...

Excerpt from:
UN Special Committee on Palestine Report Addendum 1
3 September 1947

Text of the Balfour Declaration

Foreign Office
2 November 1917

Dear Lord Rothschild,

I have much pleasure in conveying to you, on behalf of His Majesty's Government, the following declaration of sympathy with the Jewish Zionist aspirations which have been submitted to, and approved by, the Cabinet:

"His Majesty's Government view with favour the establishment in Palestine of a national home for the Jewish people, and will use their best endeavours to facilitate the achievement of this object, it being clearly understood that nothing shall be done which may prejudice the civil and religious rights of existing non-Jewish communities in Palestine, or the rights and political status enjoyed by Jews in any other country."

I should be grateful if you would bring this declaration to the knowledge of the Zionist Federation.

Yours sincerely,

(Signed) Arthur James BALFOUR

Article 22 of the Covenant of the League of Nations

1. To those colonies and territories which as a consequence of the late war have ceased to be under the sovereignty of the States which formerly governed them and which are inhabited by peoples not yet able to stand by themselves under the strenuous conditions of the modern world, there should be applied the principle that the well-being and development of such peoples form a sacred trust of civilization and that securities for the performance of this trust should be embodied in this Covenant.

2. The best method of giving practical effect to this principle is that the tutelage of such peoples should be entrusted to advanced nations who by reason of their resources, their experience or their geographical position can best undertake this responsibility, and who are willing to accept it, and that this tutelage should be exercised by them as Mandatories on behalf of the League.

3. The character of the mandate must differ according to the stage of the development of the people, the geographical situation of the territory, its economic conditions and other similar circumstances.

4. Certain communities formerly belonging to the Turkish Empire have reached a stage of development where their existence as independent nations can be provisionally recognized subject to the rendering of administrative advice and assistance by a Mandatory until such time as they are able to stand alone. The wishes of these communities must be a principal consideration in the selection of the Mandatory.

5. Other peoples, especially those of Central Africa, are at such a stage that the Mandatory must be responsible for the administration of the territory under conditions which will guarantee freedom of conscience and religion, subject only to the maintenance of public order and morals, the prohibition of abuses such as the slave trade, the arms traffic and the liquor traffic, and the prevention of the establishment of fortifications or military and naval bases and of military training of the natives for other than police purposes and the defence of territory, and will also secure equal opportunities for the trade and commerce of other Members of the League.

6. There are territories, such as South West Africa and certain of the South Pacific Islands, which, owing to the sparseness of their population, or their small size, or their remoteness from the centres of civilization, or their geographical contiguity to the territory of the Mandatory, and other circumstances, can be best administered under the laws of the Mandatory as integral portions of its territory, subject to the safeguards above mentioned in the interest of the indigenous population.

7. In every case of mandate, the Mandatory shall render to the Council an annual report in reference to the territory committed to its charge.

8. The degree of authority, control, or administration to be exercised by the Mandatory shall, if not previously agreed upon by the Members of the League, be explicitly defined in each case by the Council.

9. A permanent Commission shall be constituted to receive and examine the annual reports of the

Mandatories and to advise the Council on all matters relating to the observance of the mandates.

Mandate for Palestine, 24 July 1922 [Articles 1 to 7]

The Council of the League of Nations:
Whereas the Principal Allied Powers have agreed, for the purpose of giving effect to the provisions of Article 22 of the Covenant of the League of Nations, to entrust to a Mandatory selected by the said Powers the administration of the territory of Palestine, which formerly belonged to the Turkish Empire, within such boundaries as may be fixed by them; and

Whereas the Principal Allied Powers have also agreed that the Mandatory should be responsible for putting into effect the declaration originally made on November 2nd, 1917, by the Government of His Britannic Majesty, and adopted by the said Powers, in favour of the establishment in Palestine of a national home for the Jewish people, it being clearly understood that nothing should be done which might prejudice the civil and religious rights of existing non-Jewish communities in Palestine, or the rights and political status enjoyed by Jews in any other country; and

Whereas recognition has thereby been given to the historical connection of the Jewish people with Palestine and to the grounds for reconstituting their national home in that country; and

Whereas the Principal Allied Powers have selected His Britannic Majesty as the Mandatory for Palestine; and Whereas the mandate in respect of Palestine has been formulated in the following terms and submitted to the Council of the League for approval; and

Whereas His Britannic Majesty has accepted the mandate in respect of Palestine and undertaken to exercise it on behalf of the League of Nations in conformity with the following provisions; and

Whereas by the afore-mentioned Article 22 (paragraph 8), it is provided that the degree of authority, control or administration to be exercised by the Mandatory, not having been previously agreed upon by the Members of the League, shall be explicitly defined by the Council of the League Of Nations;

Confirming the said Mandate, defines its terms as follows:

Article 1
The Mandatory shall have full powers of legislation and of administration, save as they may be limited by the terms of this mandate.

Article 2
The Mandatory shall be responsible for placing the country under such political, administrative and economic conditions as will secure the establishment of the Jewish national home, as laid down in the preamble, and the development of self-governing institutions, and also for safeguarding the civil and religious rights of all the inhabitants of Palestine, irrespective of race and religion.

Article 3
The Mandatory shall, so far as circumstances permit, encourage local autonomy.

Article 4

An appropriate Jewish agency shall be recognised as a public body for the purpose of advising and co-operating with the Administration of Palestine in such economic, social and other matters as may affect the establishment of the Jewish national home and the interests of the Jewish population in Palestine, and, subject always to the control of the Administration to assist and take part in the development of the country.

The Zionist organisation, so long as its organisation and constitution are in the opinion of the Mandatory appropriate, shall be recognised as such agency. It shall take steps in consultation with His Britannic Majesty's Government to secure the co-operation of all Jews who are willing to assist in the establishment of the Jewish national home.

Article 5

The Mandatory shall be responsible for seeing that no Palestine territory shall be ceded or leased to, or in any way placed under the control of the Government of any foreign Power.

Article 6

The Administration of Palestine, while ensuring that the rights and position of other sections of the population are not prejudiced, shall facilitate Jewish immigration under suitable conditions and shall encourage, in co-operation with the Jewish agency referred to in Article 4, close settlement by Jews on the land, including State lands and waste lands not required for public purposes.

Article 7

The Administration of Palestine shall be responsible for enacting a nationality law. There shall be included in this law provisions framed so as to facilitate the acquisition of Palestinian citizenship by Jews who take up their permanent residence in Palestine.

Letter from Dr. Theodore Herzl to

M. Youssuf Zia Al-Khalidi
Wien-Watering
Carl Ludwigstrasse 50
19 March 1899

Excellency,

I owe to Mr. Zadok Kahn's kindness the pleasure of having read the letter which you addressed to him. Let me tell you first of all that the feelings of friendship which you express for the Jewish people inspire in me the deepest appreciation. The Jews have been, are, and will be the best friends of Turkey since the day when Sultan Selim opened his Empire to the persecuted Jews of Spain.

And this friendship consists not only of words—it is ready to be transferred into acts and to aid the Moslems.

The Zionist idea, of which I am the humble servant, has no hostile tendency toward the Ottoman Government, but quite to the contrary this movement is concerned with opening up new resources for the Ottoman Empire. In allowing immigration to a number of Jews bringing their intelligence, their financial acumen and their means of enterprise to the country, no one can doubt that the well-being of the entire country would be the happy result. It is necessary to understand this, and make it known to everybody.

As Your Excellency said very well in Your letter to the Grand Rabbi, the Jews have no belligerent Power behind them neither are they themselves of a warlike nature. They are a completely peaceful element, and very content if they are left in peace. Therefore, there is absolutely nothing to fear from their immigration.

The question of the Holy Places?

But no one thinks of ever touching them. As I have said and written many times: These places have lost forever the faculty of belonging exclusively to one faith, to one race or to one people. The Holy Places are and will remain holy for the whole world, for the Moslems as for the Christians as for the Jews. The universal peace which all men of good will ardently hope for will have its symbol in a brotherly union in the Holy Places.

You see another difficulty, Excellency, in the existence of the non-Jewish population in Palestine. But who would think of sending them away? It is their well-being, their individual wealth which we will increase by bringing in our own. Do you think that an Arab who owns land or a house in Palestine worth three or four thousand francs will be very angry to see the price of his land rise in a short time, to see it rise five times in value perhaps in a few months? Moreover, that will necessarily happen with the arrival of the Jews. That is what the indigenous population must realize, that they will gain excellent brothers as the Sultan will gain faithful and good subjects who will make this province flourish–this province which is their historic homeland.

When one looks at the situation in this light, which is the true one, one must be the friend of Zionism when one is the friend of Turkey.

I hope, Excellency, that these few explanations will suffice to give you a little more sympathy for our movement.

You tell Mr. Zadok Kahn that the Jews would do better to go somewhere else. That may well happen the day we realize that Turkey does not understand the enormous advantages which our movement offers it. We have explained our aim publicly, sincerely and loyally. I have had submitted to His Majesty the Sultan some general propositions, and I am pleased to believe that the extreme clearness of his mind will make him accept in principle the idea of which one can afterwards discuss the details of execution. If he will not accept it, we will search and, believe me, we will find elsewhere what we need.

But then Turkey will have lost its last chance to regulate its finances and to recover its economic vigour.

It is a sincere friend of the Turks who tells you these things today. Remember that! And accept, Excellency, the assurance of my very high consideration.

(Signed) Dr. Theodore HERZL

9 781986 547048